THE Touring Musician's HANDBOOK

Bobby Owsinski

HAL•LEONARD®

Hal Leonard Books
An Imprint of Hal Leonard Corporation

Published in 2011 by Hal Leonard Books
An Imprint of Hal Leonard Corporation
7777 West Bluemound Road
Milwaukee, WI 53213

Trade Book Division Editorial Offices
33 Plymouth St., Montclair, NJ 07042

Book design: Adam Fulrath

Library of Congress Cataloging-in-Publication Data is available upon request.

ISBN 978-1-4234-9236-8

Printed in the United States of America

www.halleonard.com

CONTENTS

PART 3   THE INTERVIEWS

Preface

This book is actually the brainchild of Paul Ill, my coauthor on *The Studio Musician's Handbook*. We had planned on writing this book together until his musical schedule filled up to the point that he wasn't able to spend as much time writing as he would've liked, so I chose to continue writing the book, because we felt that it was very much needed.

Paul did contribute massively, however. Because the last time I was on the road was a few decades ago (except for a couple of small van tours on the blues circuit in the late '90s), I didn't feel I could explain the current ins and outs of a modern tour. That's where Paul jumped in, giving me the benefit of his experiences touring in the United States, Europe, and Asia. Of course, a lot of other great musicians and techs from some of the biggest acts on the planet contributed a great deal as well. Unfortunately, not all of them could be quoted or included in the interview section, because many had nondisclosure agreements with their employers.

So, thanks to Paul and to all the contributors whose lifetime of experience made this book happen.

Introduction

There are a lot of books on the market about touring. Most of them assume that you're the artist or have your own band, and attempt to show you how to book your tour and save money while traveling on the road from gig to gig. This book will certainly show you the ins and outs of being on the road, but it has another purpose. It's about what it takes to get a gig as a sideman in a touring band for a major artist, and provides a look into what happens after that.

If you're reading this book, you're probably thinking, "I know I'm a pretty good player, but I'm tired of playing in clubs on the local scene. If only I knew how to get to the next level." If that's the case, then this book is for you.

I know that many of you who are reading this have looked at the people playing in, for example, the band that supports Sting, or Kelly Clarkson, or Jay-Z, and said to yourself, "I can do that!" From a chops level, maybe you can and maybe you can't, but chops aren't all that you need to have in order to get an audition with a major artist, or even one with a regional following. Besides chops, you need the right gear, the right attitude, the right mind-set, and maybe even the right look. How to develop those attributes is just one of the things that you'll find in this book.

Even after you get the gig, keeping it and staying sane at the same time is another story. Some people are just not cut out for the road and quit after a single tour. Others hate yet tolerate it because the money is good. And even if you love it, as you get older you hate being away from family more and more. Yet, the excitement of the road, the adrenaline rush of the show, and the nonstop nature of touring itself is a hard habit to break. And if you love playing and hearing the roar of a giant crowd, it's an addiction that's hard to get over.

So check out this book and keep an open mind. In some ways, touring is just what you think it might be, and in other ways it's nothing at all like what you might imagine.

Meet the Contributors

As with most of my books, the last part of this one consists of the many interviews that I did as background for the book. These interviews are always interesting in themselves, which is why I include them and quote from them frequently along the way. *The Touring Musician's Handbook* includes a diverse range of players and techs, some of whom are currently working for some of the biggest acts in the world, while others are still climbing the ladder. Many of the following contributors have been on the road for a long time and they have a wealth of information to pass along, so be sure to read these interviews even if you already have some touring experience yourself. Now let's meet the contributors.

Grecco Buratto, guitar. Besides playing sessions with Earth, Wind & Fire, Pink, and Boyz II Men, Grecco Burrato has composed for movies and television commercials, and toured with Anastacia, k.d. Lang, Enrique Iglesias, Airto and Flora, Sergio Mendez, and Keiko Matsui.

Walter Earl, drum tech. A veteran of the road, Walter Earl has worked as a drum tech, stage manager, and tour manager for acts such as Siouxsie and the Banshees (and all their spin-off bands) and Jessica Simpson. A longtime personal assistant and sometimes tech for legendary Black Sabbath drummer Bill Ward, Walter looks into the day-to-day duties of a modern drum tech and gives us an insight into the protocol of the road.

Bob Glaub, bass. Since the '70s Bob Glaub has been a first-call bass player for superstars such as Stevie Nicks, Linda Ronstadt, Jackson Browne, Don Henley, John Fogerty, Bruce Springsteen, and many more. Currently on tour with the legendary Crosby, Stills & Nash, Bob gives us the benefit of his thirty-plus years of experience on the road.

Mike Holmes, piano and organ. Mike Holmes is unique in that he's one of the few guys in Nashville who is known strictly for his piano and organ chops. Having started his touring career with the legendary Temptations, Mike later played with a host of Nashville's finest, including Lee Greenwood, Leroy Parnell, and Delbert McClinton, among many others. Mike has a lot of experience carrying a full B-3 on tour, and he's able to share some tips on how to do it.

Terry Lawless, keyboard tech. Terry Lawless is one of the premier keyboard techs on the road today, having spent the past nine years with superstar band U2. They're not the only elite act that has utilized Terry's expertise, though. He's also been out with Don Henley, the Doobie Brothers, Bruce Springsteen, Cher, Phil Collins, and David Bowie, among others. Terry is also a great keyboard player himself, and you can find more information about him at www.terrylawless.com. A fountain of information, Terry has an abundance of useful tips and tricks, thanks in large part to his many years of road experience.

Heather Lockie, viola. Heather Lockie is a violist who loves to play with a loose federation of female string players known appropriately as The Rock 'n' Roll Strings. She has worked with a number of well-known artists, such as Spiritualized, The Eels, Dave Matthews, Linda Ronstadt, Brian Wilson, Wilco, and many more.

Paul Mirkovich, musical director/keyboards. Paul Mirkovich is arguably one of the most visible keyboardists on the planet. As musical director and keyboard player for the *Rock Star: INXS* house band, and now with *Rock Star SuperNova: The Tommy Lee Project*, Paul has been seen by millions of television viewers. But he has spent plenty of time on the road, having been the musical director for Cher, Janet Jackson, and Anastasia, as well as touring with Whitesnake, Jeffery Osbourne, and Paul Stanley (of Kiss), among many others. Paul's the perfect guy to give us some insight as to what it's like being an MD for a major artist.

Michael McConnell, guitar tech. Michael McConnell began touring in an era when the players pretty much did everything, from setting up the entire backline, mixing the sound, stage managing, and taking care of anything else that would come up. From working as a guitar tech for Mick Jones of Foreigner, Glenn Tipton and Ian Hill of Judas Priest, Aldo Nova, and Foghat, to tour managing and production managing, and mixing front of house for Taylor Dayne, Joss Stone, and Billy Squier, among many others, Michael as seen it all and lived to tell us about it.

Ed Wynne, saxophone. One of the busiest musicians in Los Angeles, sax player, singer, and songwriter Ed Wynne cut his musical teeth on the road playing for a number of '50s acts, including the Platters, the Drifters, and the Coasters, and eventually found himself as the featured soloist with the Doobie Brothers. He's currently in the same position in Al McKay's All Stars, which is an Earth, Wind, and Fire spin-off formed by its former members during the band's long hiatus.

Bobby Owsinski Bibliography

Mixing and Mastering with T-RackS: The Official Guide (Cengage Learning, 2010). In-the-box mixing and mastering is becoming the norm, and this book describes how to do just that using IK Multimedia's T-RackS 3. This book is loaded with tips and tricks useful for using T-RackS as a standalone application or as a plug-in.

The Musician's Video Handbook (Hal Leonard, 2010). Understand how the average musician can easily make any of the various types of videos now required of a musical artist, either for promotion or final product. The book also demonstrates the tricks and tips used by the pros to make a video look professionally done, even with inexpensive gear and not much money.

The Music Producer's Handbook (Hal Leonard, 2010). This book reveals the inside information and secrets to becoming a music producer and producing just about any kind of project in any genre of music. Unlike other books on production, The Music Producer's Handbook covers the true mechanics of production, from troubleshooting a song when it just doesn't sound right to getting the best performance and sound out of the band and vocalist and understanding all the elements of a typical production, including budgeting, making contracts, selecting the studio and engineer, hiring session musicians, and even getting paid! The book also comes with a DVD that looks at the various stages of an actual production and features an interview with Grammy winning producer/engineer Ed Cherney.

Music 3.0: A Survival Guide to Making Music in the Internet Age (Hal Leonard, 2009). The paradigm has shifted, and everything you knew about the music business has completely changed. Who are the new players in the music business? Why are traditional record labels, television, and radio no longer the major factors in an artist's success? How do you market and distribute your music in the new music world, and how do you make money? This book answers these questions and more in its comprehensive look at the new music business—Music 3.0.

The Studio Musician's Handbook, with Paul Ill (Hal Leonard, 2009). Find out everything you wanted to know about the world of the studio musician, including how you become a studio musician, who hires you and how much you get paid, what kind of skills you need and what gear you must have, what proper session etiquette is required to make a session run smoothly, and how to apply these skills in every type of recording session—whether it's in your home studio or at Abbey Road.

How to Make Your Band Sound Great (Hal Leonard, 2009). This band-improvement book and DVD will show your band how to play to its fullest potential. It doesn't matter what kind of music you play, what your skill level is, or if you play covers or your own music—this book will make you tight and more dynamic, improve your show, and enhance your recordings.

The Drum Recording Handbook, with Dennis Moody (Hal Leonard, 2008). This book uncovers the secret of how to create amazing drum recordings in your recording studio, even with the most inexpensive gear. It's all in the technique, and this book and DVD will show you how do it.
The Audio Mastering Handbook, 2nd edition (Course Technology PTR, 2007). Learn everything you always wanted to know about mastering—from doing it yourself to using a major facility—utilizing insights from the world's top mastering engineers.

The Recording Engineer's Handbook, 2nd edition (Course Technology PTR, 2009). Revealing the microphone and recording techniques used by some of the most renowned recording engineers, this book will tell you everything you need to know to be able to lay down great tracks in any recording situation, musical genre, or studio.

The Mixing Engineer's Handbook, 2nd edition (Thomson Course Technology, 2006). This is the premier book on audio mixing techniques provides all the information needed to take your mixing skills to the next level, along with advice from the world's best mixing engineers.

PART 1

THE MAKING OF A
TOURING MUSICIAN

CHAPTER 1

The Mystique of Touring

I n many musicians' minds, there are two events that signal a change in their musical life from "wanna be" to "made it." The first is signing a record deal (although most musicians are cooling on that idea these days), and the other is being hired to go on tour with a popular musical entity. Now if you've already done either of these two things, you realize that a lot more goes into your musical well-being than those simple acts alone. But they are demarcation points of sorts—places where a whole new part of your musical life begins. For the musician who knows that he or she won't be in a position to sign a record deal any time soon (or even care about it, given the current music-business environment that we now live in), going on tour is the point at which the old life in the clubs ends, and a new, more exciting life begins.

The Differentiators

And what are the symbols of this new life? The tour bus is one differentiator. It's not even about the size of the venue you play in (although that's important); rather, it's more about how you get there. If you're still in a van, you're an up-and-comer, but if you're on a tour bus, you're *made*, to use a Mafia term.

Road cases are another differentiator, believe it or not. Do you have road cases with your name on them? (See **Fig. 1.1**.) If so, that means you've established yourself as a brand that others in the business can now buy into. Remembering back to a time in the '80s when the band I was in shared a rehearsal complex with the glam metal band L.A. Guns, who one day came into rehearsal a little more excited than usual, exclaiming, "We've got road cases! Now we can go on tour. Now we can get out of the clubs!" The simple act of having road cases can do that sometimes.

Fig. 1.1: A stenciled road case.

But there's definitely a change once you get on a tour bus (see **Fig. 1.2**). There's a certain amount of glamour and esteem that comes with it, at least in the beginning. But what it really means is that you begin to judge your musical status by how comfortable you are when you travel between gigs. While the bus might be cool, it's only an intermediate step; the ultimate tour is the *fly date*, which means flying out from a hub city to wherever the show is that particular night, and flying back after the gig. This is the utmost for a touring musician, but usually not even on the radar for a player that hasn't hit the tour bus level yet.

Sounds great, doesn't it? Just as with almost everything else in life, much of the perceived glamour wears off quickly. The bad part of touring is the psychological weirdness of being away from loved ones and living in an artificial environment, with 22 hours of the day to fill with anything other than your job, which can wear on you quickly. More than having musical chops or discipline, your success as a touring musician really depends on how adaptable you are and how developed your coping mechanisms are.

To most people, touring the capitols of Europe sounds great: Paris, Zurich, Munich, Tokyo—they can seem like exciting destinations to the people back home. But when you have only enough time to see the road into town, your hotel room, and the venue, you might as well be in some backwoods

Fig. 1.2: A typical tour bus.

bar in Kentucky. And when you have to borrow the support band's equipment (which might be only B-level gear by our standards) and push your own stacks of gear and luggage, there's not much glamour in that, even it you're staying in four-star hotels and you have a tour bus to get you from gig to gig.

At the end of the day, the one to two hours you spend onstage are your best part of the day, with everything else relegated to anywhere from routine to drudgery. When most musicians dream of this job, they don't appreciate the "touring" part of being a touring musician. But regardless of the negatives that come with this job (as they do with any other job), just remember this: You've made it to the next level. It's hard work but it's an experience you won't ever want to give back for anything else in the world.

People You'll Encounter

Touring is a team effort, and the musicians are only a part (in some cases, a small part) of that team. Let's take a look at the various people you'll meet on a typical tour.

THE MUSICAL DIRECTOR (MD)

The MD is the bandleader. He or she is the intermediary between the band members and the lead artist, so the artist doesn't have to engage with the players if he doesn't want to. If the drummer is dropping time, the artist might not ever look at the drummer, but she'll look to the MD and say, "Something's wrong with the drums." If there are two players who differ with one another in what or how they're playing something, the MD is the arbiter who will iron it all out.

In most pop bands, the MD may not be the best musician or singer, but he has the best handle on the form and content of the artist's music. So while many MDs surround themselves with much better players than themselves, it's the MD that knows what everyone's parts are, and even more importantly, knows when someone isn't playing the correct part. The MD is also responsible for the logistical wrangling of the band. If the downbeat for soundcheck is 2 p.m., the MD is in the coffee shop at 1:30 grabbing the drummer by the scruff of the neck and saying, "Okay, Starbucks time is over." The MD also runs rehearsals before the tour, and may sometimes do so even without the primary artist in attendance.

You get to be an MD by having the proper musical, social, organizational, and leadership skill sets. The MD must also have a personal connection with the artist and manager, since the position requires a high level of trust. Unbelievably, even though the MD holds a position of primary responsibility that requires the total backing of the artist and manager, sometimes the artist's business managers still want to confirm that the MD is worth the extra money, since the MD makes more than the other players (sometimes as much as double the amount).

THE ROAD/TOUR MANAGER

The road manager has the thankless job of handling all the minutia and logistics of the tour, securing food and lodging for everyone, checking in at the venue, getting paid after the concert, paying the bills that accumulate, and everything else in between. He also makes out the daily schedules and ensures that everything happens on time, keeps everyone working together, and even sorts out any conflicts that might arise. The road manager will also pay out all per diems and take care of any unexpected expenses that might arise.

THE PRODUCTION MANAGER

The production manager supervises the technical crew and coordinates their work with that of the venue's local crew. He also supervises moving the equipment and the staging from one venue to the next, as well as setting it up and disassembling it.

THE STAGE MANAGER

The stage manager is responsible for everything from taking care of the logistics of the stage setup to making sure that the house sound and lights meet the rider standards. On a larger tour, the job may require a full-time person, while on a smaller tour, it might require that a person like a soundman or a guitar tech who's on the tour, or even a local guy from the venue who doesn't travel with the tour, pull dual duty. You might even find that the stage manager may be the guy that seems like a glorified roadie who's helping you load in gear at a small venue. That being said, on a low-budget tour of smaller venues, a local stage manager is key to making the show go smoothly, since he knows everything about the venue and the people that work for it. Befriend him and treat him well to make your life at the venue easier.

THE CREW

Depending on the size of the tour, the crew may consist of anywhere from just one or two members to literally hundreds. Here are the most immediate members that you'll encounter.

Guitar tech, bass tech, keyboard tech, and drum tech. These folks are your personal techs and have been hired to look after your instruments. Sometimes one tech will look after several players (a guitar tech for both guitar players or for the bass player and guitar player). Sometimes a single person will tech for more than one instrument (guitar and drums, for instance). Sometimes a major player like Eric Clapton or Pete Townshend will have one tech for guitars and another for the amplifiers. We'll cover the various tech positions in more detail in part 2 of this book.

House engineer, FOH engineer, or soundperson. On a small tour, the soundperson usually takes on several jobs, from teching instruments to being the stage manager, but on a larger tour, the soundperson holds an esteemed position of mixing the front of house (FOH) sound. All artists are acutely aware that the FOH engineer plays a huge part in determining how the audience hears them, so the FOH engineer is treated and paid accordingly. Many FOH engineers have been with a successful act almost from the beginning (like Joe O'Herlihy with U2, or Bob Pridden with The Who—both who've had their gigs for over 30 years), while others are hired guns who are along only for the length of the tour. A large tour will also hire at least one dedicated stage monitor engineer (sometimes called the hardest job in show business because there are so many people to please), with many big acts hiring a second monitor engineer who's dedicated just to the artist.

Lighting director (LD). The lighting director is responsible for the lighting design and operation during the show. On a small tour, the LD may be the operator of the lighting console himself, while on a large tour he calls the cues to the various spotlight and the lighting console operators over a cue system.

THE ARTIST'S MANAGER

Most of the time, the interaction between the touring musician and the artist's manager is slim to none unless the manager decides to come out on the tour. This may occur if there's separate business to be done in the markets where the artist is playing. Many managers may come to a few shows, especially if they're local to their base of operations or are in a major media hub, but usually they're back at the office taking care of the things that managers do (like making money for their clients). On some smaller tours, it's possible that you may negotiate your pay directly with the manager, but that's usually the extent of your interaction.

Interfacing with the Artist

How much you interface with the artist depends on not only the particular artist you're supporting, but also their mood. You might be tight with the artist for weeks, and then find that he might become sullen or withdrawn and just wants to write by himself, effectively blocking you out of his day-to-day life. Don't take it personally—some artists want to be the life of the party or just one of the gang, while others don't even travel with their band. In fact, the artist might travel in his or her own bus or fly to the gigs while your drive, or even stay in a separate (and better) hotel.

Simply put, show quiet, friendly respect to the artist during the tour. You're a valued asset to their business process, but you are not their peer. During your time involved in their sphere of activity on the tour, whether on the bus, on stage, or at a group dinner, you inhabit the artist's musical, professional, and social universe as a cross between an honored guest and a highly valued independent contractor.

Let the artist set the boundaries and determine the tone of your interaction. Very rarely are artists cold or unkind to touring musicians. A casual friendliness usually prevails, but be careful not to try to get too chummy too quickly. Always be yourself and remain positive, friendly, and focused on the music. You're there to help him give the best show possible, so let him know it through your professional demeanor.

Also remember that often you're a part of the tour because

someone else (usually the MD) hired you, so you represent that person, too. Do all you can to ensure that the artist has the most positive and valuable experience possible. Ultimately, they take final responsibility for the tour's outcome. It's their name, not yours, that's up in the bright lights, so do your absolute best to make certain they're proud of your contributions. You want a glowing smile on their faces after each show, but most importantly, you want the artist to come away from each experience very happy with you and extremely proud of your musical contributions to their life's work.

Finally, also consider anyone associated with the artist (like a spouse, family member, boyfriend or girlfriend, guest, driver, personal assistant, or staffer) as an "artist," too. Treating them lightly can bring the scorn of the artist down on you!

A History of the Touring Musician

We think of the touring musician as being a recent phenomenon brought about by the big money of the record business, but musicians have been touring for at least a thousand years. They certainly weren't as organized or comfortable, and they didn't have the support staff that today's musical star tours with, but they traveled from city to city, town to town, burg to burg nonetheless. Let's take a brief look at the history of the touring musician.

The Troubadours

If you look at it from the standpoint that making music in a different village every day was their job, the European troubadours of the High Middle Ages (from AD 1100 to about 1350) can be considered to be the first touring musicians. Originating in southern Italy, troubadours spread to France, Germany, Spain, Portugal and Greece, with each troubadour being both a composer and a performer who sang mostly love songs derived from poems (like much of our music of today). During this time, the rules of poetic composition became somewhat standardized and were written down, which enabled troubadours to exchange and embellish each other's songs. The downfall of the troubadours was primarily caused by the spread of the Black Death (the bubonic plague), which killed a third of the European population at that time.

The Minstrels

While the troubadour did some traveling, it was generally in an area limited to a certain locality (much like a regional band of today). It wasn't until the beginning of the Renaissance period in the 14th century that the true traveling musician, the minstrel, came on the scene. Minstrels differed from troubadours in that they performed songs that told stories of distant places and of real or imaginary events. The minstrels performed both in the palaces for royalty and in the streets for commoners, and became the chief source for news of the day. It can be said that touring musicians and street performers of today share in the same tradition as the minstrels.

The Touring Orchestras

The great European composers of the 15th and 16th centuries assembled orchestras (that were similar to the orchestras of today) to perform their compositions, but they didn't begin to travel to perform their music until the nobility built retreats away from their palaces and main residences. Still, it was expensive to send an orchestra to an out-of-the-way place, and the logistics were oppressive.

That all changed in the United States in 1884, with the opening of the Trans-Continental Railroad. Travel suddenly became convenient, efficient, and cost-effective and opened up new performance opportunities for the orchestras. As the railroad gained in popularity, costs dropped to the point where an overnight sleeper compartment in a train was even cheaper than a stay in a hotel. But innovation does have its unintended side effects, and musicians traveling by train suffered then from exactly the same problems facing today's touring musician. Weather delays frequently meant that they didn't arrive on time, and being in close contact with so many people on the train made it easier to contract more illnesses.

That being said, touring orchestras soon became a hit because for local promoters they were a cheaper alternative to hiring a local orchestra, since the hall rental costs for the local orchestra's rehearsals were eliminated. This occurred because touring orchestras hit upon the idea of offering a selection of three different programs, which meant that the orchestras knew their show inside out (very much like the touring musicians of today). As a result, an orchestra could offer as many as five different concerts over the course of three days instead of having to use some of that time to rehearse a totally new program in each city.

Fig. 2.1: *The John Philip Sousa Band*

By 1902, everyone from the New York Philharmonic, New York Symphony, Boston Symphony, New York Opera, and even the John Philip Sousa Band were touring, because the train now made it easier to travel from city to city and therefore make it possible to efficiently fill open dates that could never be filled before (see **Fig. 2.1**).

The Wild West

At the heart of 19th century show business were the medicine shows, which traveled the country offering a program of music, comedy, and novelty acts as a way to sell their tonics and elixirs. At the same time, Wild West shows featured a combination of music and trick riding as a way of sustaining a dying culture just a bit longer. These were essentially seat-of-the-pants operations that had no advanced promotion, with the show suddenly appearing in town and making a lot of noise to attract attention, then frequently leaving town directly following the show.

Vaudeville

While Wild West and medicine shows tended to be performed in the local town square or park, a new form of entertainment arose that was based in the indoor comfort of the local theater. Vaudeville originally began around 1880 as entertainment for a built-in audience of farmers while they waited to have their wheat milled, and it eventually grew into a circuit of 4,000 theaters across the country that provided almost unlimited work for the traveling musicians of the time.

Gigs in vaudeville were divided into three categories.

• Small time was centered on small-town theaters and inexpensive theaters in larger cities, and could be considered the equivalent of playing in a local nightclub of today. This part of the circuit was either a training ground for new performers or a place for has-beens trying to eke out a living.

• Medium time was a better class of theaters in medium to large-size cities, and was the equivalent of the large regional club (the kind that books national acts today) or theater gigs of today.

Fig. 2.2: *The Orpheum Theatre in Seattle.*

• Big time encompassed the best theaters in the major cities, which were approximately the same stature as the arena gigs of today. The best of the big-time gigs was the Orpheum Circuit, consisting of 56 theaters in 45 cities located all over the country. Fifteen Orpheums still exist in cities from Vancouver to Los Angeles to Omaha to Wichita to Boston and New York, and they run shows involving touring musicians to this day (see **Fig. 2.2**).

Although we tend to think of vaudeville as a short-lived fad, it was actually with us for about 50 years and provided what amounts to the beginning of our touring sophistication as well as much of the showbiz jargon still in use today. Terms still in use include *red carpet treatment* (a red carpet was laid from the dressing room to the stage so the performer wouldn't damage an expensive costume by walking in it on the bare floor), *corny* (unsophisticated comedy that was "stuck in the corn"), a *tough act to follow* (performing after an act that was enthusiastically accepted by the audience), and *knock 'em dead* (doing a show that went over well).

So what killed vaudeville? As has happened a few times before and a few times since, the fall of vaudeville was a result of a change in the public's taste more than anything else. Movies were always part of a typical vaudeville bill (they were placed at the end of the show after the headliner), so the newly invented "talkie" movies (movies with sound) didn't directly contribute to its demise as is so widely thought. And as so frequently happens, the musicians and performers that adapted to the next evolution of entertainment continued working, while those that didn't found work in other fields.

The Big Band Era

The vaudeville era gave way to the era of the big bands in the late 1920s. Although big-band jazz had its start in New Orleans in 1898 at the end of the Spanish-American War, the swing era of the '30s and '40s became a fertile time of work for touring musicians since most big bands consisted of between 12 and 25 players (eventually settling upon a more or less standard 17 pieces). During this time, bandleaders and soloists were as revered as the musical stars of today, and their work gained a wider audience due to live performances on radio and appearances in motion pictures. As a result, ballrooms throughout the country played host to a wide variety of touring big bands (see **Fig. 2.3**).

Fig. 2.3: The Glenn Miller Orchestra

The Bebop Era

Fig. 2.4: *Charlie Parker*

After the Second World War, jazz turned from the era of the large band with fixed arrangements to smaller ensembles that were based around an improvisation called "bebop." Smaller groups had the advantage of accruing lower costs when traveling, but the music was mostly accepted only on the American coasts and selected inland cities such as Kansas City and Chicago. The Midwest did produce numerous bebop legends such as Charlie Parker (see **Fig. 2.4**) and Lester Young, but they had to move to New York or Los Angeles to make it (not much different from today, actually). Bebop attained greater acceptance in Europe, which remains a fertile ground for jazz gigs to this day.

Country Music on the Road

Fig. 2.5: *Hank Williams— one of the early country music stars.*

Country music has gradually evolved from a combination of traditional folk music of the Deep South and the Appalachian Mountains into a multivariety art form appreciated around the world. Because country music crosses so many subcategories (Western swing, bluegrass, gospel, honky-tonk, rockabilly, outlaw, Bakersfield soul, country rock, country pop, and the new alternative country to name a few), it has long been a haven for the musician with a hankerin' to play some music on the road.

Although culturally and historically centered in Nashville as a result of the *Grand Ole Opry* radio show (which is based there), country music knows no geographic lines, with strong contingents in every state and large followings in Canada, Australia, South America, South Africa, Germany, Ireland, and even the Soviet Union. Indeed, country musicians are some of the busiest road dogs of any musical genre (see **Fig. 2.5**).

The Chitlin' Circuit

Fig. 2.6: *The Apollo Theater—a major stop on the Chitlin' Circuit.*

The Chitlin' Circuit was the name given to a string of venues in the South, Midwest, and Northeast that were safe for African American entertainers to perform in during the time of racial segregation in the United States (from the late 1800s to about 1960). The circuit proved to be an important training ground for music legends like Count Basie, George Benson, Ray Charles, Duke Ellington, the Jackson 5, B.B. King, Otis Redding, Muddy Waters, James Brown, and Ike and Tina Turner, among many others (see **Fig. 2.6**).

Baltimore is viewed as the heart of the Chitlin' Circuit (named after a soul food item called chitterlings that consists of stewed pig intestines), which stretched down to Texas and Florida, into the Midwest to Chicago, Detroit, and Gary, Indiana, and north to New York City, and eventually west to St. Louis and even San Francisco. During a time when long-distance travel was still uncomfortable, it was nothing for a performer on the Chitlin' Circuit to do a string of one-night stands that often spanned a distance of as much as 800 miles. As if the travel aspect weren't brutal enough, hotels and restaurants were segregated, adding severely to the discomfort of touring.

Touring in the '50s and '60s

Beginning in the 1950s and lasting through the 1960s, gigs became more plentiful as new clubs, auditoriums, and arenas across the country were eager to feature shows with the latest trend in music, which was rock 'n' roll. As rock began to evolve and become more popular, a new gigging source—the many colleges and universities across the country—cut down on the distances one had to travel between gigs, as long as the tour was properly managed.

Having the hottest music show on television (*American Bandstand*), Dick Clark expanded into touring with his Parade of Stars (see **Fig. 2.7**), a grueling three-month tour of one-nighters that featured everyone from the wimpiest pop stars of the generation to soon-to-be superstars like the Rolling Stones, Roy Orbison, and the Supremes. Although they were traveling by bus, the accommodations were hardly as luxurious as those of today's models, resembling a school bus in that there were no bathrooms or recreational features.

Fig. 2.7: *Dick Clark's Parade of Stars.*

This was also a time of limited international travel. Thanks to the British Invasion, UK acts with chart-topping singles poured into the country, only to be shocked at the vast expanses between venues in the States after being used to the relatively shorter drives between cities in Europe. Only American superstars like Bill Haley in the '50s, and later the Beach Boys and the stars of Stax Records (Otis Redding) and the Motown Review (all of their star acts) ventured to the other side of the pond. Instead, hit acts of the time mostly resorted to sending promotional films to another country (we now call them music videos) in lieu of touring.

The '70s—the Turning Point

The modern era of touring really began in the '70s, as the era of big business began to dawn on the music industry. After the famous Woodstock Festival in 1969 (see Fig. **2.8**) proved that rock could easily draw tens of thousands (even hundreds of thousands) of fans, the music promoters, agents, and managers everywhere lost their innocence as the dollar signs began to flash before the eyes of entire industry. As the money flowed in greater and greater amounts, celebrity musicians on the road began to demand more comfort in their travels, and the customized

Fig. 2.8: *Woodstock—a turning point in the music industry.*

tour bus was born as a result, soon to be followed by the private jet and what we know today as the "fly date" (see chapter 4).

Every decade since then, concert production has grown more sophisticated and extravagant, with major superstar tours requiring larger, more specialized crews and as many as 20 full-size trailers to haul the gear from venue to venue. But unless you're in the star strata that can command a Gulfstream IV for transportation, few aspects of touring have changed since the early 1900s. Depending on your rung on the musical ladder, you're either staying overnight with fans or friends and eating as cheaply as you can, or staying in a hotel room and eating the free continental breakfast or the catered food with the crew to save your per diem (more on this in chapters 6 and 10). You travel between gigs by car, by van, or if you're lucky, on a tour bus. Your gear is safer because of the evolution of nearly indestructible road cases. You hear better onstage, thanks to excellent floor-monitor or in-ear-monitor systems. The audience can hear your performance more clearly than ever because of higher quality sound systems. And the organization and professionalism of everyone involved in the touring industry has become extremely refined as the industry has matured. But it's still essentially the same, for better or worse. And so is the personal drive and desire to do it, which has always been and always will be at the heart of a musician reaching for a better gig and a better way of life. To quote from a Talking Heads song, "Same as it ever was."

CHAPTER 3

The Touring Musician's Difference

s there a difference between the touring musician and the one who plays in local clubs? You bet there is. When you get right down to it, the club musician's main purpose is to help a venue sell alcohol, and the music is there simply as a backdrop for the liquor sales. The main purpose of the touring musician, on the other hand, is to provide musical entertainment, and while ancillary sales like alcohol are important, they're secondary to the entertainment aspect of the event.

But going on tour is so much more than that. As they would say in the organized-crime world, as soon as you become a member of the club, you're "made." There's suddenly the implication (although it may not yet be a fact) that you're successful and your personal brand has a newfound value that is much greater than before.

There's no better symbol of the touring musician than the tour bus, which has become almost iconic in American culture. It's like the mystique of the mansion on the hill to a musician or a fan. The local and regional bands show up in vans, but the "made" bands show up in a bus. And once you've made it that far, there's the elevated status of deciding who gets to come on the bus. It's better than a backstage pass or an after-show-party ticket, because it's the most exclusive part of the band's persona—the inner sanctum, so to speak. That's the feel-good payoff of gaining that status, but exactly how do you get there?

Attributes of a Touring Musician

Every touring musician has mostly the same attributes. They're demanded by the nature of the gig.

YOUR CHOPS

Despite what you may think, being a typical touring sideman is not all about how good your chops are. Sure they're important, but your ability to learn and retain the music is much more significant than your technical ability. Can you learn a body of work quickly, play it really well, and not forget anything from show to show? Can you play with confidence under unpredictable conditions? You can have the best chops in the world, but without those other traits, you'll find yourself soon sitting in the audience instead of onstage.

Most of what we do has very little to do with playing, but has everything to do with entertainment. If most musicians could keep the entertainment and sales side of the business on their minds, they would work more and they would probably do a better job in most situations. —Ed Wynne

Of course you need to have a minimum level of proficiency on your instrument, but that limit is dictated by the type of music you'll be playing and the sort of role you're asked to fill. The demands for a bass player playing with jazz-fusion keyboardist George Duke are a lot different from what folk balladeer Leonard Cohen would require from a bass player. Playing rhythm guitar behind country music star Reba McEntire requires a whole different skill set than playing guitar behind alt-rocker Billy Corgan does. Some roles require a precise technician with superior physical dexterity, while others need you to be solid and in the pocket, pushing the rhythm and nothing more. But whatever the role, you have to do it to the satisfaction of the artist, and do it so well that your performance is never a concern. Part of the reason you're hired is so the artist can feel secure in knowing that the parts you'll be playing will always sound just as the artist needs and wants them to be.

YOUR PERSONALITY

Your reputation among other musicians and people within the touring industry is what gets you hired and keeps you working, so if other artists, musicians, producers, and engineers like you as a person, like how you play, and like the feeling you bring to a rehearsal and tour, then you're more likely to get calls for work. If you were cooped up in a submarine for a while, you'd sure want to get along with the other people there with you. Obviously, touring conditions aren't even close to that scenario in most ways (although a bus is a little like a submarine in terms of how intimate the quarters are), but the fact that you are working very closely with other players, crew, production people, artists, label and agency people, and who knows who else, usually means that the easier you are to work with, the more likely you'll get asked back the next time, or at least get referred for another gig.

Playing comes first and it always will, but if you make the people paying your check uncomfortable in even the slightest way, it will come back to haunt you. Smiles and a pleasant, accommodating attitude, as well as superb personal hygiene (that's so important!) and an appropriate sense of style go really far in the touring business. There are a lot of great players available, and unless you're something unbelievably special, the people writing your check will always choose the player who is easiest to work with, all things being equal. No back talk, no sass, no snide remarks, nothing other than a wide smile and a "Tell me what you want" and "No problem!" attitude is what the people with the ability to hire you are looking for.

If you're too much of a personality yourself, you might have difficulties. That's just purely from a support musician's standpoint. I'm not saying that you shouldn't have your own personality or opinions or wants and desires, but you have to be flexible and easygoing enough to understand that it's not about you. It's just about creating a vibe, and the individual doesn't matter so much.
—Heather Lockie

How amicable are you? Can you get along with everyone else in the band? That's important, but not essential. Are you able to detach from everybody and not worry about whether you're getting along or not? That position works too. If you're a pro, you're always all about the music, so there's never an issue about getting along. You never have a bad word to say about anybody, and you avoid drama at all costs. If there's ever an argument, you know enough not to get involved or take sides.

When you're playing a gig at a bar on weekends you're might not get along with another player or crew, but you know that you'll be going home right afterward, so it's easy to tolerate someone. When you're on tour, you have to live with your co-workers in very close quarters. You're roommates because of the close nature of the tour bus, and so you have to have the ability to get along with others comfortably and without problems.

YOUR ONSTAGE DEMEANOR

Do you have the appropriate onstage personality for the artist? A lot of players get gigs because their physicality on stage is the right fit. It's not only how you look physically, but also how you look when you're playing the music. Are you active onstage? Are you a showman? That may not work for an artist who requires that you just stand there and play, but they still might want you to be passionate about the music if you can restrain yourself from not jumping around like Pete Townsend. Do you know your place onstage, and are you able to tailor your demeanor to the client? We'll cover this more in chapter 5.

YOUR GEAR

We'll go over this in detail in chapter 7, but whatever gear you bring must be not only in excellent working order, but also dictated by the type of music and the type of tour that you're doing. If storage space is limited (like when you're flying), then you might bring only your main axe (if you're a guitar player or bass player) and a backup and backline will be supplied by the promoter. Likewise, drums and keyboards will be provided by the promoter at the venue. If you're on a bus tour and you have more room, you'll bring your instrument plus whatever you need as a backup, but weight and space are almost always an issue, so the less you need to bring, the better (unless you're with a superstar). Regardless of how much or how little gear you bring on the road, it all has to sound great and work flawlessly every time.

> **Attributes of a Touring Musician**
> You have the right chops for the gig.
> You have an easygoing personality.
> Your onstage demeanor fits the artist.
> Your gear is tour ready and reliable.

A Sideman's Mind-set

If your aim is to get a road gig as a sideman for an artist or band that's already somewhat up the food chain in terms of success, you have to be aware that the mind-set of a sideman is much different than that of a member of a band. Almost all of us start our careers as band members, and since most bands are democratic, we're used to having an equal say in most decisions. Even if the band has a clear leader, we usually have at least some influence, but that's not the case as a sideman.

HAVING A BOSS

Being a sideman means that you have a boss, which may be counter to why you're a musician in the first place. Musicians are rebels at heart, and our major rebellion is against the structure of a day job. Now for maybe the first time in your life, there's a sense of structure imposed on your personal act of revolution (playing music). What's more, now there's someone telling you what to do, which can be an uncomfortable new scenario. That's a lot to take in all at once.

Indeed, in the grand scheme of things on a tour, you're way down on the totem pole of authority. At the top is the artist, and you're in a world that completely revolves around him. If it weren't for the artist, no one on the tour would have a job, and so his every whim, musical or otherwise, is always accommodated. Next is the musical director (MD), who is the surrogate of the artist in all things musical. If you want to think of it in terms of business, the artist is the CEO while the MD is the president or COO of the company. If you want to think of it in terms of the military, the artist is the officer and the MD is the platoon sergeant. The MD can have wide-reaching powers of authority and the ability to hire and fire (as in the case of the MD for an artist like Tom Jones or Christina Aguilera), or he or she can just be the musical link to the artist, fine-tuning everything at the artist's ultimate direction.

The artist's manager is another boss that you have, although not as much so if he isn't on the road with you. Many managers have full authority to do what they feel is best for the artist, which could include firing band members that aren't cutting it for some reason. In other cases, that decision is entirely up to the artist, and the manager my only carry out his or her wishes.

What this all means is that you have to be aware that you serve at the pleasure of the artist, and for maybe the first time, you have a boss.

YOUR EGO

All musicians have their own idea of how they should sound, how a song should be played, and how others should be playing it, as well as a host of other musical items both large and small. That all goes out the window when you're being hired to play someone else's songs on a tour. For the most part, you're trying to reproduce music that's already been conceived and realized, so the need for any opinion from you is unwarranted. Still, there are times when things aren't gelling and a part has to be dissected to determine where the problem is.

You've got to earn and honor rank. If you're a new hire, defer to others with more seniority. As you become integrated into the team, your time will come when your opinion may be valued. Then again, some artists won't want your ideas at all, while others will listen with an open ear yet reject every opinion. You've got to have a thick skin and realize that even if the artist listens to your idea, it might not carry much weight or be acted upon. If she listens to you and actually uses one of your suggestions, consider it a good day.

It doesn't matter how high or how low you go (in the business)—you have to approach it with a sense of humility and a sense of self-esteem, because who you are and how you're playing generally has very little to do with the gig you're on. Anybody can get a gig; the hardest part is keeping it. Most of touring is about personal interaction and making friends and not pissing people off. It has very little to do with how you play or where you went to school or any of that. It's the social aspect that's so important. —Ed Wynne

YOUR ABILITY TO TAKE CRITICISM

If you have a fragile ego, being a touring musician is not for you. The artist wants to put on the best possible show for his fans, and you're there to accommodate his or her every wish to that end. That's why if you're told you're playing too loudly, or your phrasing is off on a turnaround, or your shirt is too baggy or your hair is too slick, you want to be able to not take any of it personally and to instantly comply with a smile. You've got to remember that this is also part of what you're being paid to do.

The cooler you can be on your first tour, chances are you'll see many more tours for the rest of your life if you make a great impression on that first one. Don't claim that you know it all. There's a time to ask questions, and there's a time to just stand there with elephant ears and listen. You'll get more accomplished by listening to the right people, than you will by asking the wrong people the wrong questions. —Walter Earl

> ### A Sideman's Mind-set
> You now have a boss.
> Check your ego at the door.
> Learn to take criticism well.

CHAPTER 4

The Different Types of Tours

Not all tours are created equally, because the stature of an artist and the purpose of the tour dictate the type of tour that he or she plays. These types can be broken down by duration and venue.

Tour Duration

Tours can be divided into six general categories of duration: local shows, one-offs, fly dates, mini-tours, full tours, and corporate gigs. Let's look at each one.

THE LOCAL SHOW

Local shows are easy. You get to sleep in your own bed, you probably have a good bit of the day (at least the morning) to attend to personal matters, and you get to play in a familiar venue in front of friends and family. You can't really call a local show part of a tour (unless you happen to be passing through town during a real tour), but these types of shows are frequently used as a warm-up before the tour starts. It's a good time to fine-tune the set list, hone the production, and tighten the band. For a touring musician, it's a sweet gig, but there are never enough of them and they're all too short. Fun, though.

THE ONE-OFF

The one-off is a single show after which you return home. It can be local or it can be halfway around the world, but regardless of how long it takes you to get there, you're still playing only a single show.

The typical one-off generally entails at least some travel time (you might arbitrarily say a couple of hours), which basically means that the entire day leading up to the gig is consumed. If you can't do much else in your day but travel, do a soundcheck, and play the show, you've experienced a one-off.

THE FLY DATE

The fly date is the most desirable type of one-off that you can get, and means that you're flying on a plane out of town for the show, then returning either the same day or the next (it might take a little longer it your gig happens to be in an exotic place). You may do a series of fly dates, but you're always returning back to your home base after the gig.

Acts like Aerosmith and Madonna might do only fly dates for an entire tour, but they have private jets that can take them exactly where they need to go and bring them back to their airport hub directly afterwards without having to worry about the rigors of commercial aviation. That's not the case for the players in a touring band, who may have to fly commercially, although it may be in business or first class.

As we'll cover later in the book in chapters 7 and 9, fly dates have their own set of challenges, since there's always a limitation to the gear that you can bring and what you can carry on the plane with you.

THE MINI-TOUR

Anything that's two dates to a week on the road is considered a mini-tour. This means that you're away from home for that entire duration and don't see your own bed until you return. If a band from Boston books a show in New York and then returns directly home after the gig, that's a one-off. If it books shows in Providence and New Haven on the way and doesn't return home to Boston after either one, that's a mini-tour.

Mini-tours are inefficient and difficult to make money on because there are few economies of scale with labor and rentals. The bus, bus driver, techs, and tour managers usually cost more, since everyone would rather take a longer gig for the job security, and a short gig might get in the way of that happening. Aside from the money aspects, a mini-tour is a desirable gig, since you're not away from home for very long.

THE FULL TOUR

Once you get past a solid week out on the road, you're on a full tour. Tours can range from a week to a couple of years, in the case of a major act that has a hit album. If the album continues to sell, the tour will keep going in order to take advantage of the sales momentum, even returning to play the same city a second and third time.

Many touring musicians refuse to sleep at home even when a tour travels through their hometown, preferring to stay in the mood and rhythm of the tour. Even though it might feel good to sleep in your own bed, it can be mentally disruptive and even financially harmful, since the business manager might decide that you don't need the per diem for the day since you've telegraphed that you didn't use your hotel room. It's okay to go home to do your laundry and check in on things, though.

THE CORPORATE GIG

The corporate gig is an event at which an artist or band plays what amounts to a private party for a corporate entity. Once upon a time, this type of gig was frowned upon by some musicians and deemed to be a sellout, but as the touring business has become more mature and financially aware, the corporate gig is now the industry's cash cow. It is now commonplace for a Fortune 500 company to hire superstar acts and pay them sums that exceed their normal nightly take when on tour, but much smaller acts (including many that don't have national visibility) benefit immensely as well.

Corporate gigs are normally one-offs and fly dates, since most are so lucrative that they're worth playing even if the artist or band is not currently on tour.

Tour Durations

Local show: a single show close to home

One-off: a single show requiring travel

Fly date: a single show requiring air travel

Mini-tour: three to seven days on the road

Full tour: beyond a week on the road

Corporate date: a one-off private party for a corporate entity

---

Touring can also be categorized in terms of venues that you're playing. There are a lot more types of venues than you might think, even in these days of industry contraction.

HOUSE CONCERTS

House concerts are the most grassroots of all the different types tour dates, since the audience is small and intimate and you're playing in someone's home. This is the lowest of the low-budget tours because it's primarily acoustic music, everyone travels in a van, and in many cases, you can expect to end up sleeping at a fan's house (at least the accommodations will be homey). House concerts are more popular in some areas of the country than others, such as the American South, particularly around Nashville. Doing them is an excellent way for an artist to personally connect with her fans, and they are becoming increasingly popular.

CLUBS

Club dates are the next step up from house concerts in the touring hierarchy. The clubs could be some of the same ones you're playing now, or they could be specific concert clubs like Slim's in San Francisco or The Paradise in Boston (see **Fig. 4.1**). A club tour might be low budget, where everyone piles into a van, or it could be higher budget, with the band getting to travel in the comfort of a bus. The advantage is that there's room for more gear than when going on a house tour, but it's still limited to what can be stored in the van, the trailer, or the cargo bays of the bus. One downside is that even though you're on tour, you're still playing in clubs, which psychologically can make it seem as though your career hasn't progressed all that much as the gleam of touring wears off.

Fig. 4.1: *The Paradise, in Boston.*

SMALL HALLS

Small halls are the favorite of most performers, since the audience is large enough to feel like the excitement of a huge crowd, yet small enough to stay intimate. These venues usually seat or hold from between 1,000 and 2,500 people. Famous examples of small halls include the Agora Ballroom in Cleveland, which has a capacity of a little over 1,000, and the Fillmore in San Francisco, with a capacity of 1,500 (see **Fig. 4.2**). Another example would be just about any House of Blues club, which all have capacities of between 1,500 and 2,500.

Fig. 4.2: *The Agora Ballroom, in Cleveland.*

LARGE HALLS

Larger halls differ from smaller ones not just in capacity, but also in that the entire audience is seated (in small halls, usually only a portion of the audience sits while the others stand). Most large halls have a capacity of 2,500 to about 8,000, with the majority in the 4,000 to 6,000 range. The Gibson Amphitheater in Universal City, California, seats about 6,000 (see **Fig. 4.3**), while the Atlanta Civic Center seats 4,600. Large halls differ from most other types of venues in that they're almost always used exclusively for concerts and plays.

Fig. 4.3: *The Gibson Amphitheater, in Los Angeles.*

ARENAS

Arenas are very large multipurpose venues that seat between 10,000 and 20,000 people. Most arenas are sporting-event venues for basketball and/or hockey, with concerts bringing in only a portion of their revenue. The MGM Grand Garden Arena in Las Vegas, which seats 16,800, and the famous Madison Square Garden in New York City (see **Fig. 4.4**), which seats 20,000, are two examples of arenas that are frequently used for concerts.

The sound in most arenas is rarely optimized for concerts because of the mixed-use nature of the venue. Even though most arenas are acoustically treated (especially the new ones), an arena that works well for music is too dead for sports events, where the loudness of the crowd is especially important to the home

Fig. 4.4: *Madison Square Garden, in New York City.*

team. Since there are usually far more sports dates for a venue than there are concerts, the acoustics are compromised in the direction of sports.

Fig. 4.5: *The Hollywood Bowl, in California.*

SHEDS

A shed is an outdoor open-air covered pavilion. Because the audience is seated outdoors, sheds are usually utilized only in the spring and summer, even in the fair-weather Southern states and California. The famous Hollywood Bowl is considered a shed, and seats 17,000 (see **Fig. 4.5**), as is the Red Rocks Amphitheater outside of Denver, which has a capacity of almost 10,000.

STADIUMS

Stadium gigs are the next rung up the gig ladder, in that an act that might easily sell out an arena might not be able to come close to selling out a venue that holds two to five times as many people. Usually the smallest stadiums seat nearly 40,000, with the largest (Wembley Stadium or the Rose Bowl) holding nearly 100,000 (see **Fig. 4.6**). To ensure that a stadium date will sell out, promoters will frequently pair a number of equal-drawing high-profile acts together.

Fig. 4.6: *Wembley Stadium, in London.*

FESTIVALS

Festivals are large outdoor events that may last several days and have dozens of artists, many of them headliners, on the bill. Many festivals have secondary stages as well, and feature technical and musical gear exhibits to compliment the music. The audience can range from in the tens of thousands to the hundreds of thousands. Most performers enjoy festivals not only for the unusually large crowds to play to, but also because of the camaraderie enjoyed with the other bands. Ozz Fest, the Warped Tour, Coachella, and Glastonbury are just a few of the festivals that occur every year.

> **Types of Shows**
>
> House concert: an intimate show in someone's house
>
> Club: a small indoor venue holding 100 to 1,000 people
>
> Small hall: a venue holding 1,000 to 2,500
>
> Large hall: a venue holding 2,500 to 8,000
>
> Arena: a venue holding 8,000 to 20,000
>
> Shed: an outdoor open-air covered pavilion holding 10,000 to 20,000
>
> Stadium:– a large outdoor venue holding from 40,000 to 100,000
>
> Festival:– a large outdoor event featuring multiple headlining artists

Promo Tours

Promo tours usually consist of the artist backed by a very small band (sometimes just one other person) that might play live on the radio or television, or play in record stores for the express reason of promoting the artist's latest album release.

Promo tours have no set rules. You might fly with the artist in first class and have four-star accommodations, or you might fly cabin class and stay in less-than-stellar accommodations. In some cases, there might be no interaction with the artist until the show: you're just told when and where to show up. In other cases, you might be tied to the hip of the artist—traveling, eating, and hanging with her every step of the way.

Quite often, promo tours are fly dates and have no road travel at all. Sometimes, the road travel might consist of a rental car. Promo tours are fluid in that the itinerary usually changes in the middle as more promo dates are added, especially if the artist is hot.

International Touring

Touring beyond the borders of the United States is much different than doing a domestic tour. In the United States, travel, accommodations, currency, and audio and musical gear are both familiar and at a more or less equal level between venues. Outside of the United States, however, any one or even all of those points can vary greatly from day to day.

Gear is a major variable internationally. The United States has the longest history with many of the popular music forms, and therefore has the most seasoned crews and the best gear, although much of the world is quickly catching up, especially in the area of sound systems. Backline gear, however, is always an experiment in frustration, because what is perfectly acceptable in Romania or Thailand sometimes isn't even what we'd consider C-list gear in the States.

In terms of travel, all the cities are closer together in Europe than in the States, so the drives from venue to venue are shorter by American standards. It's common to pass through three or four countries in the same day, and major cities are somewhat closer than what we're used to. On the other hand, when English bands first come to the States, they usually freak out when they look at the itinerary and realize that they have to drive nine hours to get to the next venue, and then there's a soundcheck right away. We're used to that here, so driving in Europe is a piece of cake as long as the tour is routed well.

In Asia, you're usually playing only major cities, and you rarely venture to the hinterlands. Everything is organized and timely. In fact, it's almost military in its discipline, whereas in Europe it's loose and in the States it's even looser. And since you're almost certainly flying to your destination, that means you're at the mercy of the promoter and the local tastes with regard to the gear that's supplied.

Enthusiasm for the music is different everywhere as well, with the people in Asia being almost dignified in their applause, while the audiences in England are particularly passionate and excited about most popular music forms.

International Travel

Rental gear varies according to country.

Some crews are inexperienced compared with U.S. crews.

Shows in major cities are closer together if routed well.

Shows generally are more disciplined and organized

Audience enthusiasm varies.

CHAPTER 5

How Do I Become a Touring Musician

Does this happen when you go to a concert? You look at the person in the band who plays the same instrument that you do and say to yourself, "He's not that good. I can play at least as well, if not better." Well, maybe you can and maybe you can't, but for that moment you're caught in the same personal universe that many of us visit, and it all orbits around the same question, "How do I become like that player? How do I become a touring musician?"

Assuming that you've got what it takes, there are a lot more ways to getting that gig on the road than you might think. Let's look at some of them.

Getting Noticed

On the journey to becoming a successful touring musician, a lot of roads lead to the same place, but the way it usually works is that someone hears and likes your playing and either hires you or refers you as a result. Here are some of the many ways it could happen.

YOUR BAND

Your band is recording with a producer. The producer notices that you play really well and have a great feel, and he suggests you to another artist that he's produced or is producing who's about to go out on tour. Sometimes it might be the engineer on the session that remembers you (many in-demand engineers become producers at some point). Either way, in the course of doing your own record, you show up on the radar of someone who can hire you later.

BY REFERRAL

If you have a friend who does a lot of touring work who likes how you play, chances are that you'll get a referral from him at some point. If a player can't do a tour for some reason or doesn't get on with the client, a referral from someone established could get you in the door. That doesn't mean you'll get the gig, though; it just means that you'll get a chance to show your stuff.

BY A MANAGER

Managers and the people who work for them are influential in suggesting players for tours for their own artists, and for other managers' tours as well. Most management companies have a stable of players whom they're comfortable with, as well as a number of backups should the preferred players not be available. Management is always on the lookout for new players, though, since you can never have too many options. Besides, new and hungry players are generally cheaper, an ever-present factor in today's touring economy.

FROM AN MD

The musical director for an artist usually has more sway over the selection of a player than anyone else. Almost always a player him or herself, the MD knows what the best fit for the band is in terms of skill and feel, although the artist and management will normally have final say. Even if you're not right for the job, MDs make referrals to other MDs and artists all the time. Get noticed by an MD, and you're one step ahead in the game of getting a gig.

BY BEING SEEN

You never know who might be watching you at a gig. It could be any of the sources mentioned above, or someone who works production on a tour or in the office of a manager. If someone sees you playing and likes what he or she sees, you can get a call that's seemingly out of the blue the next time a position opens up. That's why you always have to be at your best, regardless of the venue or the size of the crowd. Even if there are only six people in the audience, there just might be that one person who can provide the referral that will lift you from obscurity.

There are two stories that illustrate this concept perfectly. The first involves a band that recently played a lackadaisical set in a Brooklyn club in front of four people. Little did they know that three of those audience members included a top manager, a top attorney, and a top booking agent. That was an opportunity lost that will probably never be regained with those three influential icons. The second story involves Van Halen, which played their Starwood Club show in Hollywood like it was Madison Square Garden in front of an audience of three people. One of those people was producer Ted Templeman, who signed them to Warner Brothers soon afterwards, and the rest is history.

FROM A RECORDING

Many times an artist or producer will hear you on a recording you played and will want your style or sound. It's more likely that you'll be called if the recording you played on was a hit, since everyone likes to use the people or the sound of something already successful. If that happens, be happy that you've been lucky twice.

A great example of this is the fabulous drummer Brian MacLeod, who went on to play successful gigs with Tears For Fears and Sheryl Crow (even co-writing some of her hits), thanks to his work on a Madonna record.

BY REPUTATION

After you've been touring for a while, your reputation precedes you. Most touring bands are aware of who's out with other touring bands, and frequently they'll either tour together, play a festival together, or stay in the same hotel, so it's pretty easy to get to know other musicians. If you're known as a solid player who has a great attitude and is dependable, that rep gets around before you know it and you may become a first call the next time a player is needed.

BY ASSOCIATION

The old adage "All boats rise and fall with the tide" is really true. If someone within your circle of players makes it "big," they'll most likely take you with them, at least on some level. Maybe you have something unique in your sound or your feel that your player friend will remember. Maybe he just wants to help you out because you're such a cool person. Maybe it's some payback for a good deed you did long in the past. It doesn't matter as long as you're remembered and get the chance to audition—then it's up to you.

BY AN ADVERT

While it doesn't happen often, sometimes a touring gig is advertised in publications like *Musician* (the Musicians Union magazine), Craig's List, *Music Connection*, or the *Village Voice*. Most adverts are pretty bland and flat, though, in an effort to avoid the attention of the marginally qualified, who would waste everyone's time. You might see something like the following:

> Looking for drummer for out-of-town dates starting Sept. 5th.

"Out-of-town dates" is the qualifier, because it automatically eliminates anyone who can't travel. The hard date (September 5) is a giveaway about the start date of the tour.

There may be other qualifiers, as well, as in the second sentence of the ad:

> Solid, steady Max Weinberg, Kenny Aronoff style. No Terry Bozios.

This tells you that they're looking for a pocket player with great rhythm chops, and that they don't want a technician.

The beauty of an advert like this is that it could really be for anything from a show band to a major artist. That's why it's important to read all the adverts, and not to take anything lightly.

Getting Noticed

Through a recording with your band

Through a referral from a friend in the business

Through a referral from a manager

Through a referral from an MD

By being seen playing with your band

By being heard on a recording

As a result of your good reputation

Through your association with a hit maker

By answering an advert

By networking at industry events

NETWORKING

Networking can be one of the hardest things to do if you don't have a naturally outgoing personality, but it can be one of the best ways to hear about potential gigs or even to get referred. Go to places that musicians hang out, such as music conferences like South by Southwest or the New Music Seminar. You want to hang at any event where you can casually meet someone and not seem like a stalker, so hanging around a band's hotel lobby would probably be counterproductive, while a meet-and-greet or a show after-party would be ideal.

At the event, perhaps your biggest goal when networking should be to be memorable, and the way to do that is to ask questions and to make sure that the emphasis is on the person you're speaking with, not on yourself. The moment that someone (especially someone you just met) feels you're trying to get something out of him or her, they'll subconsciously turn you off. If you take a serious and honest interest in the person you're speaking with, soon enough they'll begin to ask you questions, too. If they don't, still keep the conversation centered on them. The minute you make it all about you, you'll be discounted.

What should you ask about? That's easy. How long is the tour? What was the best show they played? Which city had the best crowd? Do they have any fly dates? Are they doing any overnights? Does their touring gear differ from what they use in the studio? You get the idea.

If you don't have them already, get some business cards made up. They're cheap and well worth the money. Make sure it has your picture on it, the instrument you play, and all your contact information including cell phone number, email address, website, Facebook information, and any links you think are appropriate (to a YouTube channel or links to your music, for instance). Don't give anyone your card unless they ask for it, though. Cards are like CDs. They just fall into an unchecked pile or into the garbage unless someone is really interested in it. *Do* ask for their card, however.

Next is to have an idea of what to ask for should the opportunity arise. If the conversation does turn to you, be prepared to say, "Have you heard of any gigs opening up?" or " Do you know of anybody who is looking for someone?" Don't assume that the other person is a mind reader and automatically knows what you're thinking.

Finally, be sure to follow up after your meeting. Send an email, but again, keep it light and don't pitch them unless they respond. Then, it's okay to ask them the same thing that you would've in person. Also, be sure that your email has all of your info in the signature line. You want the person to know who you are and instantly be able to check you out if they're interested in finding out more about you before they refer you.

Networking

Go to places where you can meet players that can help.

Keep it casual and don't come off like a stalker.

Be memorable.

Ask a lot of questions.

Keep it about them, not you.

Have a business card ready, but give it only out when asked.

Ask for their card.

Know what to ask for if the opportunity arises.

Follow up but don't pitch.

Only pitch if they respond.

The Audition

Depending on how you look at it, an audition can be either really fun or so stressful that it makes you want to lose your lunch. The more prepared you are, the less likely you are to feel like doing the latter, so here are a number of things to help you through the process.

KNOW THE MATERIAL

You can be a great player, with chops that sound like they came from Mount Olympus, but the only thing that the artist or MD cares about is if you can play the artist's material well show after show. If you go into an audition thinking that you're going to wing it, you're wasting everyone's time, in which case you should be prepared for a very short audition.

First off, I want the person auditioning to play the music exactly like the record. I don't want to hear them improvise, and I don't want to hear their take on it. I want to hear them play it exactly with the right feel, just like they were playing Mozart or Beethoven. I want them to respect the music regardless of if it's Pink's music, or Cher's, or Janet Jackson's—I want them to play it exactly as you hear it on the record. Then if I ask them to change it, they're changing it from a place where I know that they know what it is, and so they can take their own spin on it after the fact. —Paul Mirkovich

Go-to guys like guitarist Peter Thorn (Melissa Etheridge, Chris Cornell, Jewel, Don Henley) will learn as much of the artist's catalog possible before the audition, going as far as to dial in the tone of the parts as well. It's a lot of work, but if you're up against another guy that did that, and you didn't, who do you think will get the gig?

The other thing is that you have to be not only better than everyone else, but you have to be different. It's basically a sales pitch. In five or ten minutes, you have to prove to them that if they hire you, they'll get more for their money than hiring anybody else. —Ed Wynne

DON'T BE LATE

Being late to an audition will just about eliminate you right from the start. It indicates that you have a reliability problem, which is the last thing anyone wants on the road. There are a lot of great players out there, and most of them are punctual and reliable. Who do you think they're going to pick?

HOW YOU LOOK COUNTS

Not only does clothing and grooming make a good first impression, but it's also important to see how you fit onstage visually with the rest of the band. It's possible to fit the bill perfectly as a player but still not get the gig because of the way you look.

As an example, an accomplished touring player I know recently got a gig with a major artist that lasted one day. He went back to the hotel and received a call saying, "We're good. Don't come back to rehearsal tomorrow." They just didn't like the way he looked against the other players in the band.

You might get rejected because you have a shaved head and so does the artist or another player in the band, and they don't want two people onstage with that look. Or you might have blond hair and so does the artist. Or you might have facial hair and no one else in the band does. Nothing personal—sometimes you just don't fit in.

I always felt that if someone is auditioning players that he's not already aware of, it's a clue that he's looking for something else besides the way you play or the gear that you have. It's a good tip that they may be looking more at how you look or at your age. I've seen that a lot. —Mike Holmes

YOUR ONSTAGE DEMEANOR COUNTS

If possible, get a DVD or watch a video of the artist and her band playing live and take notice of the onstage demeanor of the players. A lot of people get gigs because their physicality (how they look when they're playing the music) is right. Maybe the artist wants energy onstage and really likes it when a player is so into it that he's moving all around. On the other hand, some artists just want you to stand there and play, leaving any showmanship up to them. You've got to know your place, so you have to tailor your demeanor to the artist.

BRING THE RIGHT GEAR

You've got to tailor your gear to the gig. If you were auditioning for the job as the Strat player for Lynrd Skynrd, it wouldn't be a great idea to bring a Les Paul or what some perceive as a metal guitar, like a Jackson. If you were auditioning for the touring band of 50 Cent, you wouldn't bring a drum kit with the snare tuned up high for reggae or ska. Can the artist or MD imagine how you'd play with the right gear? Sure they can. But once again, if everything were equal between two players, the one who will get the gig is the one that has the right sound at the audition. That way, no guessing, imagining, or wondering comes into play. Remember, what the artist wants most is security and one less thing to worry about. Whoever can provide that gets the gig.

BE NICE TO EVERYONE

It's important that you're nice to everyone, including the crew, while you're at the audition. If these people are going to spend months on a bus with you, they'd prefer that you not to have an attitude of superiority and to be very easy to get along with. Remember, if it's a toss-up between you and someone else, the one who will get the gig will be the one that everyone believes they can live with.

> **The Audition**
>
> Know the material of the artist.
>
> Cop the sounds of the artist's records if you can.
>
> Don't be late.
>
> How you look counts; dress to impress.
>
> Your onstage demeanor counts.
>
> Bring the right gear that fits the artist's music.
>
> Be nice to everyone, especially the crew.

CHAPTER 6

How Much Will I Get Paid

One of the first questions that you'll have either before or right after the audition is, "How much will I get paid?" If it's your first touring gig, you probably don't care so much about the income as long as you get the job, but a few months down the road it will start to bother you if you settled for a lot less than everyone else in the band did. That's why it's a good idea to know what the expected pay range is, and when, where, and how you'll receive it.

Normal Pay Rates

Touring musicians are usually paid a weekly salary or a flat fee for the tour. You're a hired gun, so you'll be paid the same whether you play two shows or seven shows in a week. If the tour does well and makes some extra money, you may be paid a bonus at the end, but it's never safe to count on that happening given the current economics of touring, and the world in general. The Musician's Union usually isn't involved, except in the case of some orchestral players. Most of the time, you're strictly an independent contractor doing a work for hire job.

Most pay rates are negotiated in $250 increments. An entry-level artist might offer only about $750 a week, but it could easily go as low as $500, plus per diem (which we'll cover later in the chapter). You might decide to take a gig like that just to get your foot in the door, or the money might be immaterial because you might want to build a long-term relationship with the artist.

A midlevel artist may pay between $2,000 and $2,500 a week, again negotiated in increments of $250. If you're good enough to play with a superstar act, you can expect a weekly salary of between $10,000 and $20,000. Some superstars may even pay their sidemen with a piece of each gig, which could mean a substantial financial upgrade. This usually applies only to longtime support band members, though.

There's more to what you're getting paid than your weekly salary. You will be compensated for rehearsals, but they're paid at a lower rate than the tour, usually half or even one-third of the tour rate. An artist might say, "We need you from February 1 to Feb 14. The tour starts on the 7, and there'll be three rehearsals somewhere between the 1st and the 5th. We're going to pay you $4,000 for the two weeks." You can break that down a lot of ways, but one way to interpret it is that you're making $1,000 for the rehearsal week and $3,000 for the tour week.

Other things you want to know are if you'll be paid extra for doing radio promos or for clinics while on the road, and if so, how much per performance? These may be duties that fall under the category of what you're being paid a salary for, but maybe not. And although this is almost never an issue on any legitimate tour, if you have the slightest inkling that something doesn't feel right in your discussions with management, you'll want to confirm that all transportation and hotel expenses you incur are covered.

You'll want to find out if you'll receive extra compensation if you do extra band duties. Can you act as the artist's keyboard tech as well as play in the band in order to make some extra dough? If it saves the tour a body to house and feed, management might consider the extra compensation well worth it. As you move up the touring food chain, doing double-duty will be less of an issue, since you'll be compensated more highly and there are dedicated people for each position.

Remember that everything is open to negotiation, but some managers may say, "This is all we have. Take it or leave it." If that's the case, then other factors enter in to the decision you ultimately make. You'll have to ask yourself questions like, How much do I like the music? Will doing the gig help my career? Do I like the people involved? Is the travel easy?

One helpful way to approach negotiating pay might be to decide what your personal minimum pay would be. What's the least amount of money that you'd leave all your own projects for to go do this job? Conversely, what's your "ideal" rate of pay? Some advocate upping your ideal rate of pay by a third when you begin negotiating with an employer, and then feeling out how that is for the employer. If you're clear with yourself about your minimum rate for the job, then this process is painless and even kind of fun. —Heather Lockie

Pay Rates

You'll receive either a weekly rate or a flat fee for the tour.

You'll be paid either at the beginning, middle, and end, or just at the beginning and the end of tour.

You will occasionally be paid a bonus at the end of the tour.

The Musicians Union usually isn't involved.

Your pay rate will be negotiated in $250 increments.

Per diem is a big part of your pay.

You might be paid to assume extra tour duties.

You might be paid for extra promo or clinics.

Everything is negotiable.

Per Diem

Per diem is a Latin term for "per day" that refers in touring to the daily amount of money you're paid to cover your food expenses. The rate may be as low as $25 a day for an entry-level act, and can range up to $100 per day or more for a superstar act. An international tour may pay higher per diems than a domestic one, because it's so much more expensive to eat because of the exchange rate these days. Or then again, it might not.

How and when you're paid a per diem seems to be at the center of most salary negotiations, because there are a lot of different situations to cover. For instance, will you get per diem for the travel days? Does per diem start the day you leave town? What everyone aspires to is that your first travel day is a per diem day. Even though you might spend the better part of a day traveling to Australia, you're per diem might start only after you land. If you ask for the per diem for the fly day, prepare for management to say, "Wait, we paid you for a week of rehearsals, and the fly day is part of that week."

An unfortunate new trend in the industry is to tax your per diem, which means that you're receiving a lot less than advertised. This issue is a by-product of the business being run more and more by accountants. That being said, it is a negotiable issue and something you should fight hard against.

It's become very corporate these days. Today, everything is pretty strictly business; back then it was a lot looser. I don't mean it was unprofessional, but you had a lot more freedom in how to get something accomplished. Now you're touring with a tour accountant who's watching every penny and it's all business. —Michael McConnell

Right around the end of the '90s, touring really became more corporate and seemed to be taken over by accountants. —Terry Lawless

Although you get paid for rehearsals, some artists might pay a per diem for rehearsals as well, but it all depends on what tier of the business they're in. It's all negotiable, and the looseness of the per diem depends upon how tight the tour budget is.

You can make quite a bit more money if you don't actually spend your per diem. Many touring musicians I know save that money, eat simply and prudently on tour, and end up with a lot more money in their pockets at the end of it. —Heather Lockie

---

Per Diem

Is an amount of money to cover daily food expenses

Is usually paid either weekly or biweekly

Might be paid on travel or off days

Might be taxable

Might be paid for rehearsals

Can mean extra money if saved

How You're Paid

Getting paid is pretty easy. The business manager of the artist will deposit a portion of your total salary directly into your bank account at the beginning of the tour, again halfway through the tour, and the balance when the tour ends. You always have money in the bank before you leave so you can relax and not worry about being able to pay your bills.

In some cases, management will even buy gear for you if the artist feels that it's required for the tour (like custom-fitted ear buds for in-ear monitors), but that's all negotiable. Only if management is a bit on the sketchy side will you have to hunt them down after the tour to get paid.

Per diems are paid out of the tour managers "float." They'll pay you in as large a lump sum at one time as they think you can handle, because feeding it out every day is a lot of work. This usually means that you'll receive your per diem weekly, but it could very well be every two weeks instead.

Ways to Save Money

Many players try to save as much of their per diem as they can by living as frugally as possible. This means eating the catered meals with the crew, taking some extra breakfast items from the continental breakfast in the morning to last you through the day, or visiting the supermarket from time to time.

YOUR BUDGET

The first time you hit the road, you might not consider a personal budget if you're making more than you're used to and the tour is part of an adventure. As a result, you'll find that you have a lot less left at the end of the tour than you were prepared for. That's why most touring veterans work on a daily budget, which helps to keep their spending habits in line.

Many touring musicians use their per diem as the yardstick for their daily budget, saving it up for a few days so they can splurge a little on others. Others make it a game to see how little they can actually spend, and will use all sorts of tricks to keep as much of the per diem in their pockets as possible, as you'll see next.

VENUE CATERING

One of the best ways to save your per diem is to take advantage of the catered meals as often as possible. Many gigs have catered food made at the venue, and most of the time it's really good (it's not pizza and donuts) and is prepared by a chef with a great deal of care. In fact, a lot of venues take pride in their catering, and the larger ones might even have a separate dining room that's lined with memorabilia from past tours. Many of the larger tours carry their catering with them.

Although they're primarily prepared to feed the crew, the band is included as well. The thinking here is that if you get to the venue at 2 p.m. and soundcheck is at 5 p.m., you don't have time to go out to get something to eat. Many players actually look forward to this, because you get to mingle with the local crew and pick up some of their social flavor, which is a lot easier over a meal (even if it is quick). In the event that you have guests, you can ask the caterer if they can dine with you, although you will probably be charged a nominal fee if they can accommodate you (which sometimes they can't because there's not enough food left over).

YOUR HOTEL

Another way to keep you budget on track is to eliminate extra hotel charges. Every hotel that you stay in is one big trap of extra charges, so it's best to be aware of what places you'll be staying before you end up using your entire per diem on a charge you could've easily avoided.

The first is the hotel restaurant, which is always way more expensive than the choices you can find if you walk only a little way from the hotel, assuming that you're in the middle of a town or city. Room service is another big expense that can be easily avoided. If you feel like eating in your room, order take-out or delivery. It will be end up being a lot faster, a lot cheaper, and probably be better food too. The minibar is another definite no-no if you're trying to save some dough. It may be convenient, but it's way overpriced and the charges add up in no time after you breach that "I'll only have one" barrier. While you might have no other choice because of time, finding a laundry or dry cleaner off the hotel premises can also save you big-time. Check the phone book for something within walking distance. Chances are that it's the same one the hotel uses anyway.

It's less of an issue than it was before since everyone has a cell phone these days, but don't make phone calls from your hotel room, because their prices are exorbitant. When traveling internationally, it's best to buy an unlocked cell phone in the States that will work in the country you're traveling to, then buy a prepaid SIM card (see **Fig. 6.1**) at a 7-Eleven (they're everywhere) when you get there. That way you can make local calls without incurring the huge roaming charges that come with U.S.-based phones. If you can get an Internet connection, you can also use Skype to make and receive calls home.

You also have to know to shut the roaming off on your cell phone when you're overseas, so you don't come home to a $3,000 bill. The best thing is to go to Orange, Vodaphone, or Virgin Mobile and get a one-time "burner" phone. You just use it for that tour, and then pull the SIM out when the tour is over. —Walter Earl

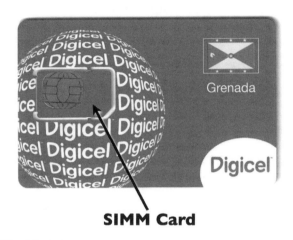

SIMM Card

Fig. 6.1: A store-bought SIM card

SEND IT HOME

Finally, if you've accumulated extra money that's burning a hole in your pocket, send it home by buying a postal money order from a post office or 7-Eleven and simply dropping it in an envelope for snail-mail delivery. It's not as fast as using Western Union or doing a bank transfer, but it's way cheaper and more convenient. If you want to get it there faster and you're nervous about the U.S. Postal Service, then use FedEx. Sending money back from overseas is a lot trickier, since it's a hassle to find a bank. The Thomas Cook Foreign Currency Exchange (thomascook. com), which is similar to our Western Union, is a safe and easy way to send it (see **Fig. 6.2**).

Fig. 6.2: Thomas Cook Foreign Currency Exchange

EXCHANGE RATES

Speaking of overseas, one of the easiest ways to lose money is through the exchange-rate transfer fee when that is incurred when converting dollars or any other currency to another currency. The easiest way to avoid this fee is to convert as few U.S. dollars into local money as possible. Trying to figure out what the right amount to convert will be is always a shot in the dark, but if you multiply your daily budget amount by the number of days you'll be in country, that will give you a general ballpark idea. And while you're at it, try not to use your credit card if you can, since you'll be charged an elevated exchange rate and a currency-exchange service charge on top of it. Buy everything with cash to stay on budget and avoid extraneous charges.

Ways to Save Money

Have a daily budget and keep to it.

Eat the hotel continental breakfast and the catered food at the venue.

Watch out for extra hotel charges for phone, room, minibar, and laundry services.

Be careful of exchange rates and overseas credit card usage.

Turn the roaming off on your cell phone.

Buy a prepaid SIM card.

Use Skype when possible.

Other Considerations

There are other things besides money that players take into consideration before accepting a tour gig. A big one is how many overnights there might be. An overnight is a night that you have to sleep on the bus instead of in a hotel room. Many people have trouble sleeping on a bus, which can have a serious impact on other areas of your life, not just your playing.

The other thing you might want to know is how many off days you have. Playing four gigs a week is a lot less work and stress than playing six days out of seven. The number is an uncertainty, however, since many off days get filled in as the tour progresses.

Questions to Ask

Here is a list of questions to ask regarding money before you take that gig.

- When and how will I be paid?
- How much is the pay for rehearsals?
- How much is the per diem?
- Is there a per diem for rehearsal dates?
- Is the per diem paid on travel days?
- Is the per diem taxed?
- Is there any compensation for doing extra band duties?
- Does per diem begin the day I leave town, or does it begin the day of the first gig?
- Will I be doing any radio promo or clinics? If so, will I be compensated?
- Are there any overnights on the bus?
- How many days off are there?

CHAPTER 7

Your Gear

The gear that you use on tour is mostly determined by two things: the artist's type of music and the method you are using to travel. A gig with Adam Lambert might require a completely different setup than one with Carrie Underwood because of the style of music inherent to each artist. A good example is guitarist John 5, whose rig with Marilyn Manson wasn't anything like the one he used on the KD Lang tour. That being said, some players' touring rigs can stay pretty much the same because they've designed them to be versatile, and to produce the types of sounds required across a wide range of music styles. Furthermore, some players are hired for the sound they bring to a tour, like the great bassist Leland Sklar, who uses the same gear regardless of whether he's out with James Taylor or with Stevie Nicks.

The particular mode of transportation when you travel also determines the type of gear you choose. If you're lucky enough to do fly dates, you'll probably be restricted to a limited amount of gear that you can bring because of the high cost of shipping large, heavy pieces as airline cargo. In this case, you take only what's necessary, and the promoter will be responsible for providing the rest of your gear as specified in the contract rider for the gig. A guitar player or bass player might take only his or her main axe on the plane in a soft case so that it can be stored in an overhead bin, while a drummer might bring a favorite snare. A backup instrument might fly in cargo (see below about ATA flight cases), or the promoter might supply that, too.

For an arena tour, where the gear travels by truck from venue to venue, you can bring your entire rig plus any backups you think you might need. In this case, most gear is loaded into flight cases, although the cases may not need to be the same quality as the ATA cases needed for flying (more on this in a bit).

If you're doing a bus tour where the gear has to fit in the cargo hold of the bus, once again you're limited by the space available. Usually that means you travel with your main instrument and a backup, and the same for amplifiers. Drummers will bring their kits and extra snare drums, pedals, cymbals, and heads.

Everything Must Work

Whatever instrument you play, you need the right gear for the job and it must be in tip-top playing condition. There's no place for temperamental gear or gear that needs a lot of maintenance, since you have to be certain that it will function the same way and sound the same for every single show.

Having well-maintained gear is essential for the musician who's serious about touring. Everything is expected to work perfectly, with no tuning problems, no extraneous noises, and no intermittents (unexplainable crackling and on/off operation). The better everything works and sounds, the better you'll look in the eyes of the people around you on the tour and the better show you'll do.

If you're a drummer, this means that at minimum you have new drumheads on all drums, your drums are in tune, and the pedals are in good working condition. If you're a guitar player or bass player, it means your instrument is properly intonated so that it plays in tune anywhere on the neck, none of your cables are crackling, and your amp doesn't buzz or hum (and make sure that your tuner is working, too!). If you're a keyboard player, you must have all the patches, samples, transpositions, sequences, and MIDI assignments programmed so they're instantly available and there's no wait between songs. And, like guitar players and bass players, your gear and cables must work flawlessly as well. If you're a horn player, it means that none of your valves or keys stick, and the instrument makes no extraneous noises when being played.

These are the things that are not only expected, but are also required just to get in the game. Your instruments must sound great, first and foremost.

AND YOU NEED A BACKUP

You must have a backup for every critical item so that in the event of an onstage failure, you can switch to it in a moment's notice. Guitar players and bass players need at least a second instrument and a second amp or head. Drummers need a second snare, hi-hat, and kick pedal. Keyboard players usually have a secondary way at getting to the sounds they need, either virtually through a computer or through a device like a Muse Research Receptor (see **Fig. 7.1**), which runs virtual instruments and plug-ins without having to use a computer.

Fig. 7.1: *A Muse Research Receptor 2 Pro.*

As the old showbiz saying goes, "The show must go on," and the only way you can be completely sure that that will happen is to be ready for any eventuality. And this means that all essential items have a backup that can be quickly and easily accessed. There's a lot more information regarding instrument care, backups, and spares in part 2 of this book.

When you're in rehearsals, you put together a kit of spares for whatever gear you're using. The gear takes a beating, so you have to carry spares of all kinds of stuff. And as you know, a lot of the gear that's sitting on stage is backup and is not normally being used. Glen Tipton had four heads on stage, but only one was ever used and the other three were backups. —Michael McConnell

I've got two new matching Ampeg SVT-VRs, which is kind of a reissue of the old SVT. The cabinets are the four-by-ten model that are sort of a half-SVT cabinet. One of those is a spare that's set up next to the one I use, so I have them both on stage. —Bob Glaub

---

Your Gear

The artist's music and the way you travel determines what gear you bring.

Everything must be in tip-top condition and sound the same and work every time.

You need a backup piece of equipment for all critical items.

You need a utility box of spares.

For many musicians, buying road cases for their gear is a sort of right of passage. As soon as you stencil your name on the cases, it suddenly means that your stock as a musician has risen and you've made the jump to becoming your own brand.

While some players choose not to case up their gear in order to save money in the beginning of their touring career, they soon see their shortsightedness the first time a favorite instrument is damaged from falling off a ramp or loading dock. Road cases are not only worth it, but almost mandatory in that your gear always has to work, and the only way to assure that it will is to keep it protected from the frequent and many knocks of the road.

THE ATA STANDARD

Although many cases may look similar, the sturdiest (and consequently most expensive) are the ones known as ATA cases. Their design is based on an airplane parts-packaging specification (known as ATA 300 Category 1), developed by airline packaging engineers and certified by the Airline Transport Association. ATA 300–compliant cases are designed to withstand the rigors of being shipped for a minimum of 100 times, and have recessed handles that will not break during transit. The standard also details the level of quality of every piece of construction material that goes into the case, including locks, hinges, and fastening systems, and states that all rivets and screws must be noncorrosive and all edges must be rounded and have a certain level of construction quality. Because of this ATA standard, the typical road case has come to be known as a "flight case," since it's made principally to survive multiple flights.

TIP: If a road case is too heavy for one person to carry, it needs casters.

TYPES OF ROAD CASES

Road cases come in a lot of different styles and materials. As a result, all road cases are not created equal. Some are great for keeping the weather off your gear, while others are built to withstand the constant battle of the road. Let's take a look at the different types.

Fiber cases. Fiber cases are the typical drum cases that most drummers have used some time during their lives (see **Fig. 7.2**). The cases are made out of fiberglass-reinforced polyester and are very strong and rugged. While they work great for the club musician or weekend warrior because they keep the scuffs and incidental scratches off of the instruments, they're deficient for road work in several ways: there's little or no shockmounting for the instrument; they close with a nylon strap, which can be cut or lost; and their irregular shapes make them difficult to pack efficiently. This means that they usually get tossed on the top of the evenly packed square cases in the truck, where they bounce around a lot as a result. Guess what that does for the instrument? Fiber cases are also prone to caving in, should something very heavy be placed on them.

For a while, the in vogue thing here in the United States was to have cases built out of the same kind of fiber that drum cases are. They weighed about a third as much as the road cases, but they weren't as heavy duty and you couldn't fly with them because they weren't ATA approved. But if you were traveling by land and you had a crew you could trust to handle everything the proper way, they worked pretty well and lightened the load a lot. —Mike Holmes

Fig. 7.2: *Fiber cases.*

Fig. 7.3: *An aluminum case.*

Aluminum. Aluminum cases have a major advantage in that they are extremely light in weight and usually have a fair amount of shock absorption (see **Fig. 7.3**) inside. That being said, they're easy to pierce and should generally not be used for shipping purposes as a result. It's possible to get an ATA-standard aluminum case, but so much aluminum must be used to construct them that you lose the advantage of light weight that aluminum has over other types of cases.

Carpet cases. These are simple plywood cases that are covered with an outer fuzzy carpet material (see **Fig. 7.4**). This type of construction once again offers little in the way of impact relief and protection. They're heavy because the internal frame may be constructed of steel, and even though the carpet finish makes them very tough, there's not much in the way of shockmounting. Carpet cases are great for things like cables and mic stands,

Fig. 7.4: *A carpet case*

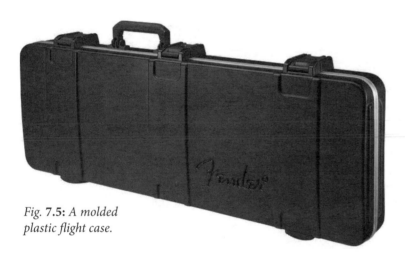

Fig. **7.5:** *A molded plastic flight case.*

but not for anything expensive that must be fully protected.

Molded plastic. Some cases are made out of molded plastic (see **Fig. 7.5**), which might be good for keeping the rain off an instrument, but it doesn't hold up well under the repeated impacts of being loaded onto a truck. Their weakness frequently is in the latches, which can break or come loose over time, and you don't see plastic cases in large sizes. And, once again, molded plastic cases may come in an odd enough shape that it won't pack easily in the truck. ATA molded cases are also rated at a standard for military electronic gear, but they're really expensive and generally custom-made.

Sandwiched material. The strongest and most commonly used road cases are the ones with sandwiched material and reinforced edges and corners (see **Fig. 7.6**), and these can be made of different materials for different types of transit. Most sandwich-type road cases are constructed in three main layers:

• An outer layer of a plastic-based laminate called ABS.
• A middle layer of three-sixteenths- to one-half-inch cabinet-grade ply wood, such as birch, poplar, or maple.
• An internal shock-absorbing foam layer that corresponds to the exact shape of the instrument or piece of gear.

The edges of the case are reinforced with aluminum extrusion, and have steel or zinc corner pieces and recessed handles and fasteners.

PROTECTIVE FOAM

There are generally two types of protective foam used in road cases. Polyurethane foam is soft and provides a gentle cushion for any delicate

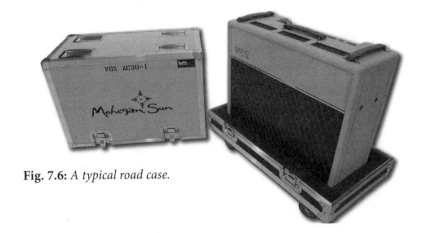

Fig. 7.6: *A typical road case.*

Fig. 7.7: *A case with cloth lining.*

item. It's usually available in one-half-inch to 10-inch thickness in one-half-inch increments. The problem is that it's so soft that it can be crushed by a heavy item, in which case a polyethylene foam is used instead. Polyethylene foam is dense and not very flexible, and the texture is almost like plastic. Frequently, it's placed under a heavy item where polyurethane simply would not last because of the constant compression. Usually, you want at least a half-inch of foam between your instrument and the outer layer of the case, although most people prefer to have one inch, for added protection.

One thing that's often overlooked with road cases is that the internal foam layer can have some negative chemical interactions with the finish of your instrument that can cause it to become dull and discolored over time. Nitrocellulose lacquer (like the type used on vintage guitars), varnish, and shellac are much more susceptible to this than are the modern polyurethane- and polyester-type finishes. The way to prevent any interaction from occurring is to make sure that your road cases have a cloth lining over the foam (see **Fig. 7.7**). Some companies use a velvetlike material layer mostly for cosmetics, but it will also protect your instrument from any finish damage from the foam. If you're buying a custom case, a cloth covering adds only a small amount to the overall cost of the case and is well worth it.

Remember, if you buy high-quality cases, they can last for your entire career on the road, so go for the best and don't cheap out.

TIP: When buying road cases, try to buy cases already in stock at your local music store or pro audio dealer, or have them made locally. The cost of shipping them can sometimes be almost as much as the case itself.

Almost every city now has a company that makes road cases, so finding one that's local should be easy.

HOW CASES GET DAMAGED

The ATA standard takes into account several real-world scenarios—like a case being dropped on one of its corners numerous times from a height of 36 inches, or bouncing across the country in the belly of a bus or truck at 70 miles an hour—but there are situations that even the toughest road cases can't take.

Believe it or not, forklifts are the main cause of road case damage. In order to pack or unpack a truck quickly, cases are frequently loaded by forklift, but there are times when you get an operator who's either in a hurry or being careless, and tries to push the cases instead of lift them. This works sometimes, but if the cases hit a barrier (like a wall) where they stop quickly, the tip end of the fork blade makes short work of any road cases and their contents as it pierces their sides with no trouble.

The next most likely candidate is a conveyer jam at an airport. If a piece of luggage jams and causes a lot of cases to suddenly back up, a case can get crinkled and deformed pretty easily if there's heavy baggage coming up behind it. That's another reason you want to spend you money on ATA cases.

And finally, although this one doesn't happen very often, you should know about it in order to erase the thought from your mind so you never try it. A drop from the second floor of a building (and even a lot less distance than that) is sure to overcome any built-in protection that any case may have. You can get away with a three-foot drop (that's in the ATA spec), but any more and you're asking for trouble.

The good thing about ATA-type road cases is that they can be repaired. Just about anything can be replaced, and the case will come back as good as new. In fact, there are companies that specialize in repairing road cases, like Mobile Flightcase Repair, although just about any road case manufacturer can do it.

I had a custom flight case made that fits both horns that's both undersized and underweight when it's loaded with everything in it. It weighs 49 pounds, which is one pound under limit, and it's also under the size limitations so I can check it like a regular bag and there are no problems. I've had that road case now for five years, and it's served me very well. It got nailed once and I had to have the top panel replaced, but even with a big gouge in it, the horns were still perfect. —Ed Wynne

Road Cases

Having good cases is mandatory for keeping your gear in working condition.

The ATA-standard case is the most rugged.

The internal protective foam provides the shockmounting.

The foam must be covered when used to surround vintage instruments.

ATA-spec cases can be damaged, but they still can be repaired.

Tour Rehearsals

S o now that you've got the gig, it's time for the rehearsals for the tour. These rehearsals are different from the rehearsals that you're used to, though, so prepare for a long day of focus and intensity unlike anything you've experienced before. For the artist, every show is expected to run like a well-oiled machine, and the rehearsal manifests that.

It's All About the Preparation

Preparation is the key to keeping your gig once you've won it. As you'll soon see, there may not be a lot of time for rehearsals, so it's totally on you to do whatever shedding is necessary so that you know the songs inside out. For some players, the preparation prior to the rehearsal is the hardest part of the entire tour. It's not so much about learning the songs as it is about being able to stop doing everything else long enough to focus on only the task at hand. This part requires a lot of mental toughness and an absolute need to overcome any attention deficit disorder (ADD) tendencies you might have.

Ideally, you'll want to come in to the first rehearsal knowing all the music that you'll be playing on the tour backwards and forwards, note for note and sound for sound, even if the artist has a catalog of 50 songs. It takes a lot of concentration and perseverance to be this prepared, so a lot of players will immerse themselves in the songs for 8 to 12 hours a day—playing, listening, charting, and learning. As you drive around in your car, you're listening to the tunes. As you're paying your bills, you're listening to the songs. As you jog, you're listening to them on your iPod. Do anything and everything, so that you know every nuance of any song that might be thrown at you.

How closely does an artist want you to learn a part? Many artists (Alanis Morrisette, for instance) give their players great leeway with the parts, allowing them to bring a bit of themselves to it, while others want every single beat like the record, right down to the ghost notes at the end of a fade. If a drum fill is supposed to be *dat, duh, did, did, dat* but you play *dat, duh, dat, di, di di*, you'll have the artist's evil eye on you even if what you just played is perfectly in time. For $5,000 a week (if that's the level you're playing at), they expect your playing to be perfect. And they'll want everything you play to *sound* just like the record as well.

That being said, everyone will make notes and charts to use during the rehearsals. These can be important tools for jogging the memory, especially if the artist has a lot of songs in the same key, or chord changes in a chorus of one song that are a lot like the changes of a verse in another. One thing's for sure, though—you want to be "off the charts" after the first rehearsal, since most artists (and players) don't like to play with readers, because they feel it inhibits their emotional connection to the music. You're not performing—you're reading. Charts can be your savior one day, but can be your crutch the next. Notes are different from charts, though, as using them might be the only way to jog your memory that you need to lay out on, for example, the first eight bars of the third song of the set and for four bars on the fourth song.

COPPING THE SOUNDS

For many artists, copying the sounds off their record is just as important as copping the notes and feel. For a keyboard player, this might not be too difficult if the synth patches or samples were saved from the session and are easily transferable into the touring setup, or if the sounds are just the traditional piano and organ. Then again, it can be a bear if the sounds on the record were done on a Korg Triton and you have a Yamaha Motif.

Matching sounds for a guitar player can be tough, too, and can take some additional time to sort out. Remember to match the sounds at the volume you'll be playing with the band, because sounds can change significantly when you go from bedroom or garage level to concert level.

Since many records have a lot of layered guitars, it's sometimes a chore to not only figure out all the parts and sounds but also determine exactly which ones you'll be playing if there are other players. That's why it's a good idea to reach out to the other player (or players) well before the first rehearsal, so you can zero in on just what's important and what isn't. That being said, don't be surprised if the parts change during rehearsal if, for example, the other guitar player decides to play the acoustic-guitar part in a song because he's also playing it on the previous song and wants to avoid an awkward transition.

The same goes for the bass parts. If all the songs have a P-bass sound and one sounds like a Rickenbacker, be prepared to have that sound ready. If a song has a part with a fuzz-bass or bass-synthesizer pedal, best to add one to your gear arsenal if you don't have it already. The same goes for the drums. If a song uses a piccolo snare, it's time to go buy one if you don't have one already.

STAGE SETUP

The stage manager or MD will usually supply you with a stage plot either before the first rehearsal or during setup (see **Fig. 8.1**) that will show the exact position you're expected to take on the stage. Your position might

Fig. 8.1: A typical stage plot.

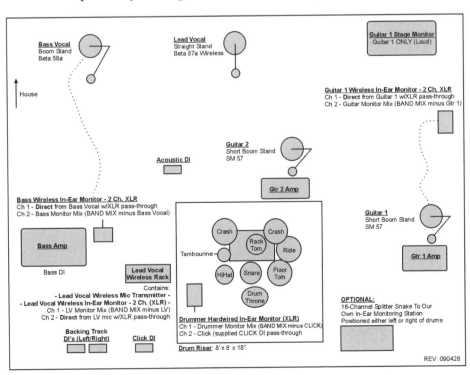

have been determined because it was visually important to the production on a previous tour, it fits into the staging in a certain way, it feels better to another player who's been with the artist for a while, or it just fits the artist's sensibilities. Whereas once upon a time, where you set up onstage made a difference as to how things sounded onstage and how some players communicated (like the bass being next to the drums), that's less of an issue today given the sophistication of today's monitor systems, which make it fairly easy to hear exactly what you want as long as you have a separate mix.

The setup for rehearsal will be tailored to the venues that you'll be playing, though. If you're playing a club tour, you'll set up really tight the way you'll be onstage at the gig, even if you're on a rehearsal stage that has plenty of room. If you're playing an arena tour, you may be rehearsing on the same stage with exactly the same production that you'll be using for the tour.

Depending on the size and scope of the show, your place on the stage can move according to the song. As the scale of the production gets larger, so might your physical contribution. If you're playing with an acrobat like Pink, for instance, you need to know that you're in the right spot at the right time so there isn't an accident when she does a flip or a dip. Be in the wrong place and get hit, it's a serious injury for both of you and the tour's over.

The idea of the rehearsals is to simulate the conditions of the tour shows as closely as possible so that you can go seamlessly from rehearsal to show. As stated above, the bigger the tour, the more likely it is you'll be using the same production, lights, sound, and stage as on the tour. The same goes for a small club tour. You might even turn most of the P.A. off on the rehearsal stage to better simulate what you'll be experiencing on the gig. If you're playing larger stages that you'll find in small halls and theaters, you'll set up so that you can acclimate yourself to the sound and feel that kind of venue provides, along with the sound and feel of the sidefills and monitors.

Rehearsal Preparation
Know the artist's catalog.

Cop the sounds.

Check with the MD or the other players about which

parts you'll be playing.

Make any notes you'll need.

Stop using the charts as soon as you can.

The Rehearsals

The number of times you rehearse is determined by the artist and the budget. The average is between three and five, but if the money is tight and most of the band has played together before, there might be no rehearsals at all. The soundcheck before the first gig may actually be the first time you play the music if the band is already established and most of the players have played previous tours together. That being said, three times seems to be the average number of rehearsals these days, considering how tight budgets are. Unfortunately, many artists who wouldn't be happy even with a couple of weeks of rehearsals still want to have a perfect machine after only three. They'll demand that you walk in and nail all the songs immediately, which is why the preparation you do before the rehearsals even begin is so important.

For this tour with CSN, we had six days of rehearsal booked, one of those were cancelled, and we didn't rehearse all that much on the remaining days, to be honest. Steven, Graham, and David have been together for forty-one years now, so they know their material and just want to get going. The first couple of gigs are almost like a dress rehearsal. A friend of mine in a fairly big band just finished rehearsing for a month before they left on tour, so it's all different. —Bob Glaub

As I said before, the bigger the production and the show venue, the more rehearsals are usually required, not so much for the music as for the production cues. It's not unheard of for a superstar act to schedule six full weeks in a dark (unbooked) arena just to get the entire show down perfectly before the first public show.

It depends upon the gig. Usually, for a major tour it's six weeks of production rehearsals, plus I'll usually work with the artist about a month before that to figure out what the show is going to be about. I'll write any incidental scene change music, segways, intros and ends, the show beginning and ending, and that kind of stuff. —Paul Mirkovich

Typical rehearsals last an entire day. It's not uncommon to begin at 11 a.m. and go to 6 or 8 p.m., or even longer if there are a lot of songs and only a few rehearsals available. If there are more rehearsals and the band has been together for a while, the rehearsals may be shorter. Either way, if you're booked for a day rehearsal, it's best not to make plans for the evening just in case.

For the Doobies, they sent me show tapes of what the other guy was doing, because they were already in the middle of a tour. I studied those and learned my parts, then we had two days of rehearsals in Las Vegas before we played our first gig with me in the band. Then we played the Hilton Theater for a couple of nights. After each night I would get notes from the guys, so I could tighten things up and figure out what they were looking for. —Ed Wynne

THE FIRST REHEARSAL

The first rehearsal is usually a half-music/half-tech day in which you get comfortable with the players and the environment and work out any technical issues, like your monitor mix and your onstage volume, with the crew. It takes a bit of time for the crew to see what kind of equipment they're dealing with and then do a proper soundcheck, so the tech part takes up the first part of the day. The time for load-in and setup isn't much of an issue, since you're usually told to load in the night before, with the stage manager or MD saying something like, "Load in at 11 p.m. on Tuesday, but rehearsal is going to start at 1 p.m. on Wednesday."

Because the tech part of the first rehearsal consists of a lot of waiting around while each player does his or her soundcheck, sometimes the artist won't even show up, leaving the MD to handle anything musical in his or her absence that might happen that day. If the artist does show up, it will usually be halfway through the day just to meet everybody for a quick chat. That being said, some artists want to run the entire set the first day, so you have to be ready for any scenario.

OTHER REHEARSALS

Rehearsals are different for everybody. Some artists want to run the entire set the first day, while others want to take it in increments. Some artists want to tackle the most difficult songs on the first day, because they might not have their set list created yet. Some artists want to work on the songs that are the most difficult for them to sing, while others want to save the more challenging ones for later. As a result, the show may develop during rehearsal. Even though it may not be a scripted show yet, they'll still want you to have all the music under your belt.

Many artists have a big catalog and, as a result, change their set lists every show to keep things fresh. That can lead to a big workload for the players. There are ways that that can be alleviated, though. For example, singer Chris Cornell's approach is, "These are the 30 songs that you should know, but don't freak. The first day, just know these five. The second day I want you to know these five, and the third day I want you to know these five. Then we'll have 15 and we'll be good for the first show."

This can work a lot better than having to run down as many songs as you can get to in one day, but if that's the way an artist wants to work, that's the way it will happen.

THE LAST REHEARSAL

The last day of rehearsal is very much like a dress rehearsal in that you're playing exactly the way you would onstage. You're going to try to run through the entire show twice just like it's a real show, with no stops even if there's an instrumental train wreck. Many artists like to have a small audience of friends for this last rehearsal to take the edge off and better simulate a show.

REHEARSAL ETIQUETTE

The rehearsal requires your utmost focus and attention. Since usually there aren't that many of them, every minute counts and so you have to be mentally present at all times.

- Staying focused is where your professionalism must shine through. It's okay to be sociable and friendly, but be sure there's no storytelling and no digressions from the task at hand. The music is the center of attention and needs to stay that way at all times.

- Follow the leader. If he or she says, "We're going to do it again," don't say, "No, we got it." On the other hand, it's not your place to say, "I think we should do it again," if the leader wants to move on, unless it's vitally important for you to address something.

- If you're addressing a particular part of another player, do it one on one in private and not on a group level. It's much appreciated if someone pulls you aside and says, "I have a feeling that you're playing the third of the second chord in the bridge, but I think it's supposed to be a minor third," rather than bringing it up in front of everyone. A public exposition of mistakes or faults is bad for morale and sometimes stops the rehearsal from moving forward.

- During rehearsal, it's unacceptable to pull a, "I have to cut out early because I have a gig tonight." The guys that do that get the eyeball roll from the artist and tour manager, but they know that the musician is in control at that point because they probably can't get a suitable replacement a few days before the tour begins. That being said, players that exhibit such inconsiderate behavior shouldn't count on a callback the next time the artist goes out on the road.

One thing's for sure. Because of the new economy, nobody overrehearses, so usually there aren't not enough of them. The key to excelling without having sufficient rehearsal time is all about the preparation you do alone, before you even get there.

The Rehearsal

The number of rehearsals varies according to the artist and budget.

The bigger the production, the more rehearsals are required.

About half of the first rehearsal is related to technical issues.

Rehearsals can run from a couple of hours to a 12-hour day.

The last rehearsal is like a dress rehearsal, where the show might be run twice.

CHAPTER 9

Preparing for the Tour

When most musicians plan for a tour, the first thing they think about is the musical gear they're going to bring. While that's important, you have to put some thought into your personal items as well. Packing a suitcase hastily can lead to overlooked articles that you'll have to buy on the road (if you can find them), which takes time and energy that might be at a premium. Here's what to think about before you begin packing so that you can be sure to take exactly what you need, and only what you need.

What to Pack

Space is always limited, so you may be able to bring only one large bag or suitcase, which determines the items that you can bring. Large, expandable duffel bags are inexpensive and can hold a lot more than even a large suitcase or travel case (see **Fig. 9.1**). One of the larger ones (either 32 or 36 inches long) can hold a surprising amount of clothing and has multiple compartments for various items, from shoes to wet articles.

Fig. 9.1: A Scott rolling duffel bag.

Generally, the clothing you bring with you will be separated into two categories: that of general clothing (gym, travel, and sleep clothing), and that of stage clothing.

GENERAL CLOTHING

Pack enough clothing to last a week, ten days at most. You'll be able to do laundry at various times during the tour, but you must have enough of everything to get you to the next laundry day. Don't forget to bring plenty of underwear, since that's the piece of clothing that everyone goes through quickly. The same thing applies to socks.

Generally, no matter how long I'm going out of town, I don't take more than a week's worth of clothes, because the suitcase gets to be too heavy and then you'll be overweight—which, depending upon the kind of tour you're on, you might end up paying yourself. I'll take sample sizes of detergent and just wash my clothes in the sink. Lay them in a towel and just walk across the towel a few times. The towel absorbs most of the moisture, so if you hang the clothes up in the bathroom overnight, they're generally dry in the morning, with the exception of jeans.
—Ed Wynne

Many road veterans prefer the feel of new socks, and will purchase new socks instead of washing them when they're on the road. While this might be a good strategy for some, don't assume that you'll always have the time to be able to do that. Besides, you're trying to save some dough, right?

I have friends who throw out socks and underwear and buy them as needed instead of doing laundry, but I'm not really into doing that. —Heather Lockie

Most of the time when we pack, it's seven pairs of black jeans and seven black shirts and maybe a couple of shirts for days off. Make sure that you can get from laundry to laundry, because there's nothing worse than wearing dirty clothes. I like to have new socks whenever I can, so I'm always buying new socks. —Terry Lawless

For your day clothes, you can get by a little longer between laundry days if you stick with basic black or any clothing that's on the dark side, which will hide tiny stains well. Anything that you wear for travel should be loose fitting and comfortable, since you may spend some long hours in one position. You also want to be prepared for all types of weather, so include at least one long-sleeve and one short-sleeve shirt, and a sweater or hoodie.

Sometimes overlooked are the clothes that you like to sleep in. Whether it's a traditional set of pajamas or a short and T-shirt, don't forget to pack a couple of sets. It's hard enough to sleep in a different or an unfamiliar bed sometimes, let alone to feel uncomfortable because you're not wearing what makes you comfortable. And don't forget those gym clothes if you work out or run.

STAGEWEAR

Some players who are naturally hip can wear the same clothes on stage that they normally wear during the day, but others pack a few changes of stagewear. You'll be under some bright lights and may be projected onto a big screen, so here are a couple of things to think about:

- If you want to wear something other than basic rock 'n' roll black, you're usually better off with rich, vibrant colors, which set up well against the stage lighting.

- Don't wear white if you're fair-skinned, because the lights can wash you out and, even worse, give you a bit of a ghostly look.

- If you perspire a lot, silk will show off the sweat. But if silk is really your thing onstage, make sure to wear something dark that won't show up the sweat as much. If you do happen to get sweat stains, a little vodka can take the stains out easily (this is an old opera singers' trick), although you might have some explaining to do to the MD.

A good trick when choosing stage clothes is to always select them under some colored lights, so you can get the feeling of how they'll look when you're bathed in theatrical lighting onstage. Also remember that it's an old showbiz tradition (and makes good business sense) that the star picks the first color, so if you know the way that he or she normally prefers to dress, you should stay subordinate to that to keep the peace. And don't forget that the shoes you wear are more conspicuous onstage than you think, so choose them carefully.

It's a good idea to check with the MD or tour manager before you pack stage clothing to see if there might be a color coordination for the band that you need to consider. For instance, at one show everyone might be in all black (or just a black shirt), and at another, you might be in white. Obviously, none of the above matters much if you're playing with an artist that requires matching stage clothes (like Tom Jones or Ricky Martin) or you're playing in an orchestra that may be touring with an artist, since orchestra members all normally dress the same.

TOILETRIES

Toiletries are important to keep you smelling fresh for not only your touring mates but also your audience when you're entertaining during an after-show party or are signing autographs. Don't forget things like mouthwash, toothpaste, shampoo, and body wash, but be sure to put them all together in a sealable plastic bag so nothing wet and messy gets all over your clothes if a tube explodes or a cap is put back on too loosely.

Here are the items you might consider bringing, because there's not always enough time to go to find a drugstore on the road:

- Nail clippers
- Q-tips
- Razors (the disposable shaving kind)
- Toothbrush
- Toothpaste
- Dental floss
- Mouthwash
- Visine or Clear Eyes eyedrops
- Airborne (There's nothing worse than traveling with a cold, so anything you can bring to fight one off is a good thing.)
- Hand sanitizer (There are germs everywhere on tour and never enough soap and water when you need it. A little hand sanitizer goes a long way toward keeping you healthy.)
- Wet napkins (Once again, when soap and water aren't available, you'll be glad you brought a stash.)
- Gold Bond powder (A lifesaver to help stifle that untimely rash.)

You have to have backups in your personal life just like in your professional one. I have backups of shampoos, toothpaste, and things like that, because there's nothing worse than getting stuck in a hotel six miles outside of town and not have anything to wash you hair with. —Terry Lawless

PRIVATE-TIME ITEMS

There are a number of personal items that should be on your list of items to pack. The first is any prescription drugs that you might need, and the second is a bottle of aspirin, ibuprofen, or other pain reliever for that raging headache that won't go away. If your sinuses tend to clog, antihistamines or nasal spray can be just the thing to help you breathe, but be careful that you don't overuse them. They can be addictive and bad for your entire digestive tract if not used in moderation.

If you sing, remember to pack anything that helps your throat feel better, be it Fisherman's Friend or an herb tea or Entertainer's Secret throat spray. And don't forget the vitamins, especially some vitamin C, to help keep your metabolism in balance and ward off colds.

Most players tour with a laptop these days in order to write, compose, and do all the things that a connected musician in the 21st century does. Having a portable keyboard or travel guitar and an amp simulator makes it easy to practice, write, or work out a new part.

Many players also like to travel with a DAW like a Pro Tools Mbox to be able to record their ideas and work on songs during their downtime. If you're carrying a laptop and speakers anyway, you're almost there.

Every time we'd reach a new venue, I set up my little Mbox recording studio and worked on a series of eight or nine songs during the course of the tour. It was very productive, since there's at least three hours between the soundcheck and show where you're waiting around the venue. —Heather Lockie

Reading material is great to help you pass the time, but if you wear glasses, be sure to bring a backup pair. Nothing is worse than not being able to see for days on end. One of those small eyeglass-repair kits with the tiny screwdriver and screws can also come in handy.

Don't forget an MP3 player, iPod, or iPhone loaded with music that you love as well as the tunes of the artist you're touring with. You never know when he's going to want to replace a song in his set with something from the catalog, so it helps to have all his tunes right at hand if needed.

And speaking of the iPhone, it's become sort of a de facto standard for musicians on the road, although any phone that can access your email is almost a must-have. Texting can get expensive, especially internationally, but email is a cheap way for the MD or tour manager to keep in touch with everyone. Not having the ability to instantly check your mail will definitely put you on the wrong side of anyone who has to physically seek you out to tell you that the lobby call time has changed.

OTHER USEFUL ITEMS

Here are a number of additional useful items to include in your away kit.

Flip-flops or water socks. There will be times when you have to share a shower with a lot of other people and the only way to prevent getting a case of athlete's foot is to have you own flip-flops.

You definitely want to take a pair of flip-flops, because the worst thing is sharing showers. You might have twelve guys that hit a shower, which means that if you don't wear flip-flops, you'll wind up with hellacious athlete's foot. A pair of Nike water socks, Aqua Socks. You've got to shower in those, because God knows what you're stepping on. —Walter Earl

Febreze. Using this fabric refreshener and odor remover is an easy way to keep your clothes from smelling bad when that ability to do laundry is just out of reach.

An extra phone charger. These become misplaced or lost so easily that it's always a good idea to have an extra. Your phone doesn't do you much good unless it has some juice. You can buy these inexpensively online at sites like meritline.com or handheld.com, but you'll pay through the nose if you have to replace one on the road.

Batteries. We (and especially we musicians) have so many things that are essential parts of our lives that run on battery power that it's important to have an extra supply of every type that you might need. It's a fact that AA and 9-volt batteries make the musical world spin around. Buying in advance can save you some money and a lot of time trying to find a place that sells them at the last minute before a show. Don't forget that extra laptop battery, especially if you have a long flight ahead of you.

A short power strip. We all travel with a lot of electronic items that have rechargeable batteries, and there are times when a couple of them need to be charged at the same time. Having your own power strip will allow you to do that when electrical outlets are in short supply.

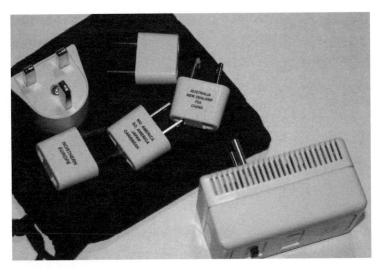

Foreign-power-conversion kit. If you're traveling to a different country, the power and the electrical plugs may be different than the ones you're used to, so you'll need a power-conversion kit (see Fig. 9.2). They're inexpensive and can easily be found online.

Sharpie markers. These come in handy in so many ways and are especially useful for signing CDs, body parts, and laundry bags.

Fig. 9.2: A foreign-power-conversion kit.

A small notebook. Sure you can take down an address or directions in the notes section of your iPhone, but sometimes using some good, old-fashioned paper is faster and easier.

Earplugs. Whether it's onstage, in a club, or on the bus, you never know when a set of plugs can save your hearing or your sanity. They're also good for keeping the maid's conversation in the hotel hallway in the morning from waking you up.

A scarf or hat. In the winter, any bit of extra clothing can keep you warm when you need it most. Beware—these seem to be the first things to get lost.

Sunscreen. You get a lot of exposure to the sun if you sit near the window on the bus or just walk around town before the show. There's nothing worse than being sore or itchy onstage, and you want to keep any chance of skin cancer at bay, so wear your sunscreen. Make sure that you select at least an SPF 30, higher if you have fair skin or burn easily. Also make sure that your brand protects against both UVA and UVB radiation and is "waterproof" if you plan to go swimming.

Insect repellant. This stuff comes in handy for those outdoor shows in the summer.

Everybody on the road knows that Avon Skin So Soft Bug Guard is one of the best insect repellants that you'll ever find —Terry Lawless

Sunglasses. This is another item that's frequently lost. Whether you wear them to look cool or shade your eyes from the sun, they're pretty essential to most musicians. Take a backup pair, too.

An LED flashlight. Ever try to find an AC outlet under the desk in a corner of a hotel room? The new LED flashlights are inexpensive (less than $10, usually a lot less), and the batteries seem to last forever. A head-mounted or "hands-free" model can also be useful when you're doing maintenance work that requires you use two hands.

A multitool like a Leatherman. Once again, if you want to cut, crimp, or screw something while on the bus, backstage, or in your room, you'll be glad you brought one. Remember to check it in your baggage if you'll be flying since it won't get past the security checkpoint in your carry-on bag.

Incense. Many hotel rooms smell, and if you can't get your room changed, your only option is to try to counteract the smell. Incense won't hide all smells completely, but it will help.

KEEP YOUR WEIGHT DOWN

If you look at all of the items above, it seems like a lot to pack—and it is. And that brings about another challenge. You want to pack lightly, because you may be charged for an overweight bag in the event that you're flying to a show. Considering that the airlines are looking for any reason to extract money from you and the tour accountant is looking to save as much as possible, packing frugally become a necessity.

What to Pack

Pack as lightly as you can, so that you avoid incurring extra baggage costs.

Take enough clothes for a week to ten days; that will get you to the next laundry.

Check with the MD to see if there's any color or clothing coordination required.

Pack plenty of underwear and socks.

Don't forget those flip-flops.

Don't forget extra batteries and chargers.

Take backups of toiletries so that you don't run out.

Don't forget the sunscreen and insect repellent.

Have a phone that receives email.

Additional Preparations

Just packing your suitcase isn't enough to be ready for the road. If you're going to be fully prepared, there are a number of other items to look into.

Fig. 9.3: An AirCanada frequent-flyer card.

SIGN UP FOR YOUR PERKS

Be sure to register for all the frequent flyer and hotel points programs that you can (see **Fig. 9.3**). Why? These are your perks for after the tour. After you do enough touring, you can accumulate enough points for free flights and hotels anywhere in the world and it won't cost you a dime. This is not only a perk for you but also for your family.

You have to get your frequent-flyer stuff and your hotel-points things together, because these are perks that you can get and share with your family when you get home. This way, your family can reap some of the benefits of you being gone, and when you share them it's a great thing. So perks like that will help you balance the family with the touring, but you have to be organized to take advantage of it. —Ed Wynne

Another reason to sign up for all the rewards programs is that it gives you some leverage when a booking goes wrong. Being a member of the club gets you priority, but being a very active member, with lots of points and a higher-status membership, really gives you priority. Just being able to change your seat from the middle to an isle during a long flight is worth it.

When you get your confirmation number, call the airline or go online with your frequent flyer number, because if you're Silver or Gold or Elite class, that's going to help you rearrange your seat assignment. You'll have priority over someone who doesn't fly as much. —Ed Wynne

CHECK WITH YOUR DOCTOR

If you're traveling overseas, it's a good idea to check in with your doctor before you go. That way you'll find out if there are any travel advisories, and you can get immunized for an affliction that's uncommon here, but plenty common in the country you're visiting. Many of the diseases that were long ago conquered in the United States are still raging around the world. Even if you don't get sick, you don't want to be a carrier and bring it home to your family and friends.

INSURANCE

Tours usually have liability insurance for catastrophes, but you'll never know until it's too late just what's covered and what isn't. That's why it's always a good idea to investigate what policies you need to cover your gear and personal possessions, so that you're adequately insured while you're on the road. If you're a homeowner, some policies might cover certain items, but then again, they might not. Speak to your insurance agent to be sure, or check out a company, like productioninsurance.com, that specializes in entertainment insurance.

Sometimes a simple travel-insurance policy is a worthwhile investment, because it can cover damage, theft, and even accidents and medical attention if you're in a foreign country. While your gear might not be covered (because most policies have replacement-cost limitations), things like clothing, laptops, luggage, and accessories are.

Do you need a separate liability policy? Is your gear covered under your present policy if you travel internationally? Does your car insurance cover any rental car you might decide to use? Call your insurance agent before you leave. You'll be glad you did, if the unforeseen happens.

Additional Preparations

Sign up for all the hotel and airline rewards programs.

Check with your doctor regarding immunizations if you're visiting a country you haven't been to before.

Call your insurance agent to see exactly what your policy covers.

CHAPTER 10

The Tour

T ime to hit the road! It's exciting, it's a bit glamorous (which wears off quickly), it's boring, and it's grueling. Here's how blues guitarist Sue Foley so exquisitely describes touring:

Life for a road musician is a cross between episodes of Survivor, The Amazing Race, and the movie Groundhog Day. It is a series of rushing, running, meeting schedules, airplanes, new countries, languages, being surrounded by strangers, carrying loads of bags and gear, trying to make it to the right place on time, being exhausted, elated, and living on rushing adrenaline. Once things settle in, it's the same grind day after day. If we didn't have written itineraries and tour managers, we would not be able to tell one town from the next, for in truth, we see very little in each town except the venues we are playing and our hotel rooms, if we're lucky enough to have them. —Blues guitarist Sue Foley

Let's take a look at the various parts of a touring day.

The Day Sheet

Your day starts with a day sheet, which is a piece of paper that outlines your Itinerary for the day that is slipped under the door of your hotel room each morning. The day sheet describes the time and place of everything important that will happen during your day, including meal and departure times, show time and venue, day-to-day itinerary info, and hints, tips, and reminders about how to prepare for the next few days (see **Fig. 10.1**).

Here's what you'll find on a typical day sheet:

Show Information

Show Date:	08/21/2008
Show Time:	9:00:00 PM
Venue Name:	Astrodome
Venue City:	Houston
Venue State:	TX
Venue Address:	123 Astro Drive Houston, TX 77077
Radio Station(s):	KIKK
Promoter:	John Promoter
Date History:	Played here in 2006. There is a 5 foot drop when loading in the back.
Revenue:	$25,000 guarantee $12,500 to pick up
Phone Gate:	713/555-1212
Contact Phone Of Promoter:	713/555-2121
Show Type:	Houston Livestock Show & Rodeo
Video:	yes, 2 screens
Production Off Phone:	713/555-4567
Load In:	8am
Sound Check:	noon
Dinner:	5pm
Doors:	6pm
Artist Show Time:	10pm
Set Length:	75 minutes
Meet And Greet:	25 people 1 hour prior to show
Comps:	20
Show Venue Capacity:	15,000
Bus Call Times:	star-midnight, band-midnight, crew-3am,
Show Other Acts:	none
Flight Info:	star departs Houston IAH Continental flt. 345@ 1:00am arrives L.A. @ 3:00am (conf#br549)
Hotel Info:	Astro Inn 124 Astro Blvd Houston, TX 77077
Presents Radio:	KIKK
Show Dressing Room:	3 rooms, showers, washer & dryer back stage

Fig. 10.1: The day sheet.

- Show date
- Show time
- Venue name
- Venue city (it might be in a suburb of a large city, so this is important)
- Venue address
- Promoter name
- Any history that the artist might have with the venue
- Venue phone number
- Promoter's contact phone number
- Production Phone Number
- Video (if video will be used at the venue, the day sheet will describe

how many screens, cameras, and so on, will be used)
- Load-in time
- Soundcheck time
- Dinnertime
- Doors-open time
- Artist show time
- Set length
- Meet-and-greet information (how many people there will be, whether it will be before or after the show, who needs to attend, and so on)
- The number of comps (free tickets) available
- Show venue capacity
- Bus call times (for artist, crew and band, if separate)
- Hotel information
- Show dressing-room information
- Other information
- Lobby call time
- Notes

The lobby call is when and where your day begins. This is the time that everyone is supposed to meet in the hotel lobby to get on the bus. It's considered selfish to be late for lobby call, because that can throw the schedule off for the rest of the day.

Everything is so organized now. You have fabulous tour managers that give you a memo every day that tells you where to be and when, when you're soundchecking, when you're checking out, when your bags are supposed to be picked up, and when your meals are. —Bob Glaub

Bus call is the time that the bus leaves the hotel for the venue, and when it leaves the venue after the show. There may be different times for the artist, the band, and the crew if they all have separate buses.

The notes section (sometimes called "other info") is a catchall for everything else that doesn't fit into any other category. Here are some examples of what you might find:

- NO food in lobby after 10:30 a.m.!

- XXX (the artist) will be doing press until 3 p.m., but you need to be at the hotel at 2 p.m. no matter what, so that we can give you the silly hats you need to wear tonight onstage.

- The bus WILL GO STRAIGHT TO THE VENUE from the hotel, so get everything that you need for tomorrow morning.

- The TOUR MGR. NEEDS EVERYONE'S PASSPORTS tonight for tomorrow's lobby call.

- There is no guest list tonight. We can do a ticket buy from the local promoter, so please LIMIT YOUR NUMBER OF GUESTS.

- Don't forget we have a 4:00 a.m. call tomorrow, so PACK TONIGHT.

- There are laundry machines on every floor of the hotel, but if you wait until we get to London, there is a Laundromat down the street from our hotel.

- Tower of Power is playing at another venue tonight one hour after our arrival. We will arrange for transportation and backstage passes . . . text me (the tour manager) now, and let me know if you wish to go.

GET YOUR APPLE ON

Be aware that anyone who has anything other than iPhones and Macs may present a problem for a tour manager (sorry, PC people, but the music business is a Mac world). The tour manager wants to be able to easily find everyone when necessary, so you've got to be available by email and check it at least three or four times a day. Texts are expensive, especially when you're traveling internationally, so email is the communication of choice. The tour manager may be in the hotel going "XXX [the artist] wants to have dinner with everyone. We're meeting at an Italian restaurant downtown," and it's no fun to have to physically find someone because they aren't "connected," while the rest of band gets the message immediately.

The Tour Bus

As stated in chapter 1, the tour bus is looked upon as the touring musician's "mansion on the hill" (see **Fig. 10.2**). It holds a unique place in the minds of concertgoers and musicians everywhere, but when it comes right down to it, it's just a way to get a bunch of people from point A to point B as comfortably as possible. The definition of "comfortable," however, is in the eye of the beholder. Let's take a look at life on the bus.

Fig. 10.2: A typical tour bus.

THE BUS ITSELF

Most tour buses are laid out in the same way. There's a small front lounge (see **Fig. 10.3**), a larger rear lounge (see **Fig. 10.4**), bunks for either 8 or 12 people (depending upon the size and layout of the bus) (see **Fig. 10.5**), a galley (see **Fig. 10.6**), and a bathroom with a shower. Most buses have a satellite television in both lounges, as well as a DVD player and sound system, wireless Internet, and maybe even an Xbox or other gaming device. Many now also have iPod docs.

Fig. 10.3: A typical tour bus front lounge.

Fig. 10.4: A typical tour bus rear lounge.

Fig. 10.5: A typical tour bus bunk section.

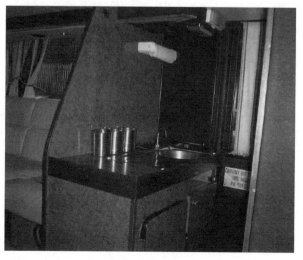

Fig. 10.6: A typical tour bus galley.

The rear lounge can usually be reconfigured as a twin- or queen-size bed when necessary. There are multiple air-conditioning zones (up to four on some buses), so you can usually find at least one area that has a temperature you're comfortable in. The bus also has a generator, so you'll have plenty of AC power for plugging in laptops and anything else that requires external electrical juice. Most bunk areas are small, but many have a flip-down television, a DVD/CD player, and their own power outlets.

If the artist and the band share the same bus, it's not uncommon for the artist to commandeer the rear lounge, even though it's supposed to be for everyone (you'd better knock before trying to enter). Someone might even sleep back there if they're claustrophobic in a bunk.

LIFE ON THE BUS

Because you share such tight quarters with from 7 to 11 other people, it's easy for tempers to fray. That's why everybody has to be on their best behavior, no matter how difficult that may be. Because you can offend someone without even knowing, you have to be extra considerate of everyone on the vehicle and respect their physical space and personal belongings. Keeping yourself and your area clean and dumping your trash at every stop go a long way toward avoiding setting off anyone's phobias or quirks.

Traveling by bus with eight other people is not something everyone can deal with. You have to have a certain type of personality to handle the intimacy and lack of privacy. The bus is close quarters, you can't walk down the aisle without bumping into someone, you can't sit alone anywhere without there being noise and a conversation, maybe someone watching a movie or listening to music. It's difficult to read, because there are too many distractions and there is literally nowhere to go except to your bunk, which is about the size your coffin will be when you die. You have to be extremely cool and conscientious of others and hope they will be the same to you, because it can be completely psychologically draining. —Sue Foley

As far as the bus goes, you never want to leave any of your stuff out in the aisle. When I started touring, they told you once to put your shoes in your bunk and if you didn't listen, the next morning they were gone. You always want to clean up after yourself, and you don't want to go to sleep leaving your beer bottles or food out. —Walter Earl

You also have to take into consideration the opposite sex if you have a male and female band. Women have different needs and a different energy from guys, which changes the dynamic of the behavior on the bus dramatically. It actually tends to get mellower as the testosterone levels decrease.

I know this is going to sound really old-school, but I always bring a book [on a tour], because sometimes when you're on the bus with a lot of people crammed in, the chances of having some kind of unpleasant discourse between band members or management or crew is pretty high. The longer you're out, the less sleep you have and the more you see the differences in personalities. It's inevitable that there's going to be a blowup. I always want to have an escape or a self-defense to get out of those social situations, which can go bad and lead you to losing your gig. Burying yourself in a book is a good way to stay out of those situations. —Ed Wynne

Is there smoking on the bus, and does that bother you? How much are recreational drugs or alcohol a part of your touring life? Can you sleep on the bus? These are the things you must ask yourself before you take the gig.

TIP: Buy a cheap pair of slippers just for the bus. They're easier to take on and off in the tight quarters of your bunk than regular shoes are.

Life on the Bus

Clean up after yourself.

Keep yourself and your area clean.

Dump your trash at every stop.

Keep your shoes and clothing out of the aisle.

Your Hotel Room

Your hotel room is a place of temporary comfort, a home base that changes every day or so. It's a place to clean up and take a shower, maybe do some laundry, catch up on your writing or practicing, and generally relax a little. But don't relax too much—you'll be there only for a short while.

HAVE A ROUTINE

The hotel gives you a bit more space than the bus does, if for what seems to be only a moment, but it's the place you're most likely to lose things by overlooking them when you leave. Just as the crew has a routine for the order in which they place the gear onstage and pack the truck with a checklist to make sure that nothing is forgotten, so you should have a routine to keep track of your personal possessions.

When you first get to your room, immediately unpack and hang up your stage clothes for the night to get the wrinkles out. If you can't get them out just by hanging them, try hanging them in the bathroom with the shower on, or ask housekeeping for an iron.

Next should be any laundry or dry cleaning that needs to be taken care of. You might have an early call the next morning, so you want to make sure that you'll have everything dry and ready to go long before then.

On most touring stops these days, you can leave a laundry bag and pick it up after the show that night, so you don't have to do your own laundry anymore. —Terry Lawless

I'll take sample sizes of detergent and just wash my clothes in the sink. If you lay them in a towel and just walk across it a few times, the towel absorbs most of the moisture. If you then hang the clothes up in the bathroom overnight, they're generally dry in the morning, with the exception of jeans. —Ed Wynne

When you check out of the hotel, the more standardized you can make your routine, the better. It's great to have a checklist, because it's too easy to leave something behind (like those phone or computer chargers). Before you leave, go back one more time to double-check that you haven't left anything behind.

TIP: When you leave the hotel, take along a matchbook, a business card, or a piece of hotel stationery with the hotel's name, address, and phone number in case you get lost (see **Fig. 10.7**). Even if you don't speak the language, you can always show it to a cab driver to get you back.

Fig. 10.7: A hotel business card.

The Venue

It's likely that for at least some of the tour, you'll be spending more time at the venue than just during soundcheck and the gig. Even if the crew call is at a different time than the band's call, you still might have to get there at the same time because of the logistics of the tour. If the bus call for the venue is at 2 p.m. but soundcheck isn't until 5, you'll have three hours to fill.

So what do you do to kill the time? You might do some maintenance on your gear or check the Internet if you didn't have it on your bus. If you're lucky, the venue may have showers, but usually there's a fight to use them first since they tend to get a bit funkier with each use.

Every time we'd reach a new venue, I set up my little Mbox recording studio and worked on a series of eight or nine songs during the course of the tour. It was very productive, since there's at least three hours between the soundcheck and show where you're waiting around the venue. —Heather Lockie

Maybe there are no showers at the venue and the bus isn't there for you to hang out and relax in because it can't get down the narrow street. You might find you have a day room at the hotel that's only a block or two away. A day room is a hotel room that's booked only for the day and must be vacated by 6 p.m. Sometimes you're able to walk around town to kill some time, but other times you're asked to stay close to the venue.

Usually, between soundcheck and the show you'll have a catered meal at the venue, as we discussed in chapter 6.

If the venue does have showers (most venues besides clubs do), what it might not have is a supply of towels—or if it does, they may be limited. As a result, there's a protocol for taking showers that's almost as important to know as anything else on the tour—namely, the artist showers first. If for some reason you can sneak in front of the line before the artist, be absolutely positive there's a clean towel and plenty of hot water left for the artist. It may seem like a small thing, but nothing can incur the artist's wrath upon you faster.

And by all means, be sure to use your flip-flops (don't forget the advice in chapter 9)!

There are some courtesies that you usually learn through someone screaming at you at 2 o'clock in the morning: "Why'd you take the last towel? The artist didn't shower yet." —Walter Earl

---

The Venue
Find something to occupy you in your downtime.
Make sure that the artist showers first.
Always wear your flip-flops in the shower.

Soundcheck

Soundcheck typically occurs three to four hours before the show, which means that for an 8 p.m. show, the check will begin between 4 and 5 p.m. On a shared bill, the headliner checks first, and the opening act checks last. That way the support band can keep their gear set up for the show, although it's usually placed in front of the headliner's gear. The headliner's soundcheck can take as long as an hour, while the support band may get only 15 minutes or less (sometimes only a single song).

Soundchecks themselves can vary a lot. Often, they can turn into a rehearsal to work out a new part or to revisit a part in the show that doesn't feel right. Sometimes they can even turn into a writing session, with the artist trying to fine-tune something new she's working on. Then again, many artists prefer not to do a soundcheck, once they're confident that the onstage sound is consistent from show to show.

The first and primary focus is for the artist to get her monitor mix right, and then longtime band members or the MD get next priority. After that, everyone else onstage gets to hear what they need to according to the various levels of priority, if there's time.

The soundcheck is about making other people happy, and the sooner you realize that it's not about you, the less frustrated you're going to be. Socially speaking, soundcheck can be a really good way of losing your job. I've seen it happen to guys that complain too much. It's starts with, "I can't hear myself," and then it escalates to include other people's stage volume and how they have to turn down for you, and it can spiral out of control really quickly from there. Then you throw in the fact that everyone is jet lagged, you've had three hours of sleep, and you're halfway around the world, and you can see how tempers can flare in no time. —Ed Wynne

High up on the priority list is the FOH engineer, since the sound will vary from venue to venue. He'll normally want to hear your softest song and your loudest song, or anything else in the set that he feels can help him gauge the acoustics of the room better.

With regard to making your soundcheck go smoother, it pays to be friends with the monitor engineer more than anyone else on the crew. He's the person that will determine what your mix is like, so getting on his good side can mean he'll spend just a little extra time on you if you need it. The monitor engineer is also the person with the most stress onstage, since his is the most unforgiving and most unheralded job in show business. The musicians notice only when their mix is bad, and never when it's great. A kind word can go a long way to helping your mix be exactly what you need it to be for every show.

The most important thing you can do for soundcheck is to make friends with the monitor engineer. If you make friends with him, he's going to go out of his way to make sure that you're happy, Then, it doesn't matter if you show up at soundcheck or not. Buy him a bottle of Jack, thank him for working so hard, grieve with him that he's underpaid (because they always are), and that will go a long way. He'll go way farther for you than if you show up at soundcheck going, "I can't hear myself!" —Ed Wynne

Other than that, check your instruments, make sure your song notes are where you can see them, and relax a bit before the show.

TIP: Wear earplugs for the beginning of soundcheck to protect your ears from loud blasts of feedback.

> ## Soundcheck
>
> It's for the artist first and foremost.
>
> It's for the FOH engineer second.
>
> It's for the longtime band members after that.
>
> Then it's for you (if you're lucky).
>
> Making friends with the monitor engineer can help
>
> improve your mix considerably.

The Show

The show is the payoff. It should be magical, it should be fun, and you should have an out-of-body experience that transports you to an alternate universe. The other 22 hours of the day simply lead up to these 2.

The show can be rigid from night to night and hardly ever change, or it can be flexible, depending on the artist. An iconic band like Black Sabbath may play nearly identical shows every day. They know they're going to walk 20 paces to the stage from their four trailers, play these 14 songs from 10 p.m. to 11:49 in a specific order, and if Tony Iommi (the guitar player) stretches out, they're going to cut a particular song. It's basically the same routine every day. Very few bands have that luxury, though, and many even get bored with an unchanging routine and intentionally try to mix it up every few shows. Then there are the situations in which you're forced to be a lot more fluid from day to day.

As an example, at a major festival in Switzerland, my friend bassist Paul Ill played a festival where the artist had serious throat problems. In order to do the show, the band had to transpose the entire set down by as much as a fourth. The stress level was really high as a result, because the way they had to play the music was different from how they had learned it originally. To make matters worse, all the other bands who played at the festival were there checking them out, which only added to the stress.

I've been playing with Cher for 20 years and some of it is really silly music, but I always tell people in the band whenever we start to wander before a show, "Let's play this show like it's the 4th or 5th time we played it, not the 105th. Let's go back to square one and play it like we learned it. There's someone that comes in every night that can't wait for her to sing "Gypsies, Tramps, and Thieves," and as silly as that may seem to you or me, they've waited their entire life to hear her sing that song. And if there's a bunch of shit all around it and it doesn't sound like the song they expected, they're going to go home disappointed. So that's the attitude you have to have when you go to play pop music. There's an art to how the producer and the artist put the song together and you have to respect it, unless they've asked you to change it. You can't just change it up because you're bored or you think that your idea is better. —Paul Mirkovich

After the Show

After the gig, you're naturally wound up. You have this magnificent rush of energy that you get from the show and it's hard to come down from it. Your natural inclination is to want to party or do something to take the edge off. Maybe someone wants to take you to a club to jam afterwards, or there's an impromptu party in a hotel room. That's a classic scenario showing why some road warriors have drug and alcohol problems.

If this is your first time out on the road, you'll certainly want to experience of little of that, but remember that a touring musician's first loyalty is to his boss (the artist) and the music. Try to temper your energy and enthusiasm, be professional, and get some sleep instead. You probably won't sleep well on the road, so you have to get more than you would normally in order to stay rested. This is a good time to use the extra hours to maintain your relationship with your people back home.

After a show, instead of sitting up and knocking down a dozen beers and watching movies, you should just go to bed because you need to rest to do your job well. You have to understand when it's a school night and what you need to do to stay sharp the next day. —Terry Lawless

After a few weeks on the road, you start to get weary. After a couple of months, you're constantly tired in a low-level sort of way. Sure, you may be getting enough sleep, but it's a restless, uncomfortable sleep that silently wears on every fiber of your being. When that happens, it's easy to give up on any health routines you might have, and just want to survive. That's when you have to be more vigilant than ever, before you slip into some nasty habits that can stay with you for the rest of your life.

YOUR DIET

One of the first things to get out of whack is your diet. Junk foods are never good for you, but they can be especially hazardous on the road. Fast food can not only add some unwanted pounds but also play havoc with your voice (the additional dairy products like cheese and mayonnaise are special culprits). Mayo alone can add 200 calories to a dish, and anything with a cream sauce adds even more. You're better off to ask whoever is serving you to hold it or put it on the side.

The most important thing is to eat healthy, and it's so easy not to in our situation. There are snacks and sodas around all day, and you have a number of choices for meals because most (of the bigger) tours are very well catered. So you need to watch your diet and keep your weight down. A lot of guys put on weight when they go out on tour because they eat a lot at meals and eat a lot after the show. —Terry Lawless

Watch your diet. That's a big deal. I've seen so many guys that would go out on their first tour and come back a year later, and they'd gained 40 pounds. You get to the venue at about four o'clock, and backstage there's going to be catering, it's going to be good, and you're going to pig out. As you know, musicians are not known for their self-control. —Mike Holmes

The best time of the day for your biggest meal is lunch, since a light dinner works best to prepare your metabolism for the show. At lunch you usually have a great variety of dishes to choose from, with a lot of healthy alternatives. Be on the lookout for ethnic restaurants, because they usually have many healthy alternatives rich in vegetables and protein (like tofu). If possible, remember to substitute brown rice for white; it's healthier for you.

Try not to eat after the gig. The only kitchens that seem to be open late are the ones that feature deep-fried food. When you eat a grease-laden meal before you go to bed, there's no chance for your body to work it off. The calories can really add up after a few nights a week of postgig fried-food gorging. If you must eat after a gig, keep it light and healthy.

You have to stay away from eating pizza every single night, unless you're 25 and still have the metabolism of a hummingbird. The older you get and the better shape you can keep your body and mind, the better you're going to perform and play.

One of the things that's great about being on the road is that you travel to great cities and you can eat a lot of great food and you can go out and party with your friends every now and then and have a really great time. But you can't do that every night, because you're going to end up fat and lazy and not in very good shape. Eventually, it will take its toll no matter who you are.
—Paul Mirkovich

On the bus, apples and peanut butter on whole-wheat bread provide a good source of protein, carbohydrates, vitamins, and roughage, and will help you save your per diem. It's easy to get dehydrated, so drink lots and lots of water and substitute fruit juice instead of soda whenever you can. Healthy alternatives like protein bars, dried fruit, trail mix, and nuts are easy to take with you to snack on, and the more fresh fruit you can eat, the better.

I also take PowerBars or some kind of nutritional bar on the road with me, because you can't depend upon other people for your sustenance on the road. I've been stuck before when we've missed our flight and nobody had any money for food, so I learned never to go out on the road broke. Don't let anyone stick you on an eight-hour bus ride on a sit-up bus with no food and no water where they're telling you, "We can't stop because we don't have the time. We're going to miss soundcheck as it is." While that may be true, you have to take care of yourself, so when you get on the bus, take a bottle of water and a couple of PowerBars. If they stop for lunch, great. If they don't, you're still covered. —Ed Wynne

Finally, take a shower whenever the opportunity presents itself, since it doesn't come often enough.

KEEP EXERCISING

It's easy to get into a rut when you're on the road. A little bit of jet lag, a few nights without enough sleep, and the subtle mental and physical beating that your body takes from being away from home for long periods can wear you down to the point that you'd much rather sit around than keep in shape. Resist that urge and keep a regular exercise routine regardless of how tired you feel. You'll feel a lot better when you get those endorphins flowing, you'll have more energy, and you'll keep that excess weight from accumulating, too.

Yeah, eat well, watch your diet, and exercise. I go to the gym at the hotels we stay at three or four days a week. You have to stay active and walk around the cities you visit rather than sitting in your hotel room and being a vegetable. —Bob Glaub

The ticket for me has always been a bicycle. I keep a mountain bike under the bus in the baggage compartment, and that's what saves me. In the last 20 years for me, it's become a package deal: "No bike, no Mike." When the other guys are holed up in the hotel all afternoon, I'm out pedaling. —Mike Holmes

Staying Healthy

Get enough sleep.

Watch your diet.

Eat your biggest meal at lunch.

Don't eat after the show.

Keep exercising.

Traveling Internationally

Traveling domestically can be tough, but international travel takes the hassle factor up a notch. While most of the same issues regarding touring apply, there are some nuances that require some explanation.

YOUR PASSPORT

If you're traveling anywhere outside the United States, you must have a passport. This wasn't always the case, though. Before 9/11, you could travel almost anywhere in the Western Hemisphere with just a driver's license and a birth certificate. That all changed with the Intelligence Reform and Terrorism Prevention Act of 2004, which stipulated that travelers need to carry a passport or some other form of "secure" document to get back into the United States. Forget about the other secure documents—just get the passport.

HOW TO OBTAIN A PASSPORT

If you're trying to obtain your first passport, you must apply in person either at one of the many post offices around the country (usually the bigger ones) or at one of the federal regional passport facilities, which are located in many major cities. Check www. iafdb.travel.state.gov for a list of offices where you can apply.

You'll need two 2-inch-by-2-inch passport photos, which you can obtain from a number of places in your town (check the phone book or online), though you may be able to obtain them for about $10 at the facility where you apply. You must supply a proof of U.S. citizenship and another proof of your identification. This means you should bring a certified birth certificate (no photocopies) or certificate of naturalization and a driver's license (and your old passport if you have one that's expired). If you don't have your birth certificate, you must contact the Country Recorder or Registrar of Birth in the county where you were born. You can also go to www.vitalcheck.com to order your birth certificate online. The current price is $75 for the passport book and a $25 execution fee.

Make sure that you obtain a "passport book"—and not a "passport card." The card does not apply to air travel and can be used only between the United States, Mexico, Bermuda, the Caribbean, and Canada.

Passport turnaround time is usually six to eight weeks, although many people receive them sooner. You can also apply for expedited service, which can bring the turnaround time down to 7 to 14 days and will cost an additional $60 plus FedEx charges. It's also possible to make an appointment at the nearest regional passport facility for same-day issuance, but keep in mind that it takes three to four hours just to make the passport, so get the earliest appointment time you can. If you can't travel to a facility, there are a number of passport services that can expedite your application so you can receive it in as little as 24 hours, but that'll set you back as much as $300 on top of the application fee. For more information right from the source, go to www.travel.state.gov/passport.

To Obtain a Passport

You need proof of U.S. citizenship, personal identification, and two 2 x 2–inch photos.

You can apply online or in person.

The normal turnaround is six to eight weeks.

An expedited passport cuts the waiting time to one to two weeks.

Make an appointment at a regional passport facility if you need it within 24 hours.

You can use a passport service, but it will cost extra.

KEEP IT CLOSE

Your passport is your most important document when traveling overseas and is coveted by thieves everywhere. That's why you have to keep it as close to you as possible at all times, which means don't leave it in a bag and always keep it on your person no matter what.

Many tour managers will ask for a scan of your passport in order to have all the needed information to obtain a new one in the event that yours is lost or stolen. If you scan your own passport, don't leave the image on your computer, since it's just the thing that crooks and terrorists the world over are looking for. Losing your passport scan might not prevent you from getting in and out of the next country, but it can cause you problems down the line when some breach in security is attributed back to your passport!

The first thing is you don't want to put your passport in your bag—you want to carry it close to you at all times. You never want to lose control of your passport when you travel. Many tour managers will ask you for a scan of your passport but a lot of guys are rightfully paranoid about that. If you do take a scan of your passport and it's on your computer, a lot of bad things can happen in the event that you lose your computer. So if you scan it, keep it on a server or a flash drive, but not on your hard drive. —Walter Earl

Your Passport

You need one for all international travel.

Keep it on your person at all times.

Remove any scans of your passport from your computer.

DEALING WITH JET LAG

Jet lag occurs after traveling by air across several time zones in a short period of time, which causes your body's circadian rhythm (your internal clock) to be thrown out of sync with the local time of your destination. It's generally believed that for every time zone you cross, you'll need a day to recover. This means that a flight from New York to London that crosses five time zones will take five days for you to reestablish your regular sleep patterns.

Symptoms of jet lag include insomnia, irritability, indigestion, and disorientation in the days following arrival, which makes it one of the hardest parts about traveling internationally and it is universally dreaded as a result. The worst part is that if you don't deal with it immediately, it can drag on for a week or more. Here are a few tips to help you deal with jet lag, but keep in mind that everyone reacts differently to it, so the remedies may or may not work for you.

- Take some melatonin. Melatonin is a hormone that has the key job of controlling the body's circadian rhythm, and it plays an important role in when we fall asleep and when we wake up. Many veteran travelers suggest taking a .5 mg melatonin supplement an hour or so before bedtime for the first three nights after you arrive at your destination in order to ease the jet lag effects.

- Adjust your sleep and wake-up times. If you are traveling eastward, trying going to bed one hour earlier and getting up one hour later starting a few days before you leave. If you are traveling westward, do the same, but adjust the times one hour later.

One tip that I have is the way I dealt with jet lag. I'd wake up at like four or five in the morning and go jogging. It was hard because your body is really tired, but if you can get yourself up and moving and get your circulation going, you can see a bit of the town you're in as well as help yourself adjust to the new time much more quickly than normal. That kind of exercise really energizes you so you're more capable of dealing with the jet lag. —Heather Lockie

- Limit your nap time. If you must nap after you've arrived, try to keep it to about an hour at a time. Napping for longer periods will just prolong your adjustment period.

- Limit your diet. During the flight, avoid alcohol and caffeine, drink lots of water, and eat lightly. This is really difficult, especially on a long flight, but it makes your adjustment time shorter when you arrive.

First and foremost, you can never drink too much water, and the less alcohol you drink on planes, the better. Even though getting a nice light buzz might seem to make the flight go faster, alcohol dehydrates you and you get off the plane feeling a little bit weak and even a little disoriented. People think it's because they're tired, but most of the time it's because they're dehydrated. —Ed Wynne

FLYING WITH GEAR

Musicians have a lot of confusion about flying with gear, and well they should. Security is tighter than ever and all of the baggage rules have changed, but it's still possible to fly with musical instruments as either carry-on or checked baggage. Here are some flying tips to keep your gear safe and the TSA happy.

- Many airlines will no longer allow a musical instrument in a gig bag to be a carry-on. This is actually a violation of the agreement between the American Federation of Musicians and the TSA, which states that you can carry one musical instrument on with you, providing it fits under your seat or in an overhead bin. Carry a copy of the American Federation of Musicians' correspondence with the TSA, which you can download from www.hornguys.com/TSALetter.pdf. (It's also on the DVD that accompanies this book.) Also, check out the article about carrying musical instruments on board at the TSA website (www.tsa.gov/travelers/airtravel/assistant/editorial_1235.shtm). Make sure that your tour manager is aware of your intention, and that the airline is contacted beforehand.

Fig. 10.8: A TSA-approved lock.

- All checked baggage must undergo at least one form of screening. Security screeners have the right to forcibly open locked baggage to complete the screening process, so leave your cases unlocked unless you want the locks broken. If a screener opens your checked baggage, they'll place a notice telling you that they opened it, and will then close it with a security seal. If you later find that something is missing, the TSA can be held responsible on a case-by-case basis, which is not much recourse if it's something that you use every night. It's always a good idea to be there when the screener opens up the case, if possible. There are now TSA-approved locks available (that appear as a traditional lock to everyone else) that can be easily opened by security screeners with a TSA master key (see **Fig. 10.8**).

TIP: If you can't be there when a screener checks you baggage, include clear written instructions in a place where the screener will notice them for repacking and handling your instrument.

- If you're able to carry an instrument on the plane, be careful that you don't store any prohibited items like scissors or wire clippers in your bag or case. These will be confiscated so they definitely need to be checked. Remember that you can only carry on one musical instrument, one carry-on bag, and one personal item, *if they allow a music instrument.*

- If you're bringing extra batteries, keep them in their original packaging. They pose a very small risk of fire (very, very small) so the TSA prefers that their terminals not be able to touch anything and keeping them in the original packaging is the safest way.

- Since August of 2006, you can bring limited quantities of liquids, aerosols and gels in your carry-on bag, but you have to observe what they call the 3-1-1 rule. That is, a 3.4-ounce (1000 ml) or less bottle of liquid put into a 1 quart clear plastic bag, and only 1 bag per person put separately into the screening bin. If you have any doubts, put them in checked luggage.

For more about airport security, get it right from the source at tsatraveltips.us. Also check out the section on flying in Chapter 16.

Flying with Gear

You're allowed one instrument carry-on.

Include understandable instructions for the screeners for handling.

Don't store any prohibited items in the case or your carry-on.

Keep batteries in their original packaging.

Get an approved TSA lock for all instruments.

Finally

Sure it's a pain, but try to keep your receipts so you're able to use them as deductions at the end of the year on your taxes. If it looks like you'll be on the road a lot, it's best to find an accountant who has experience with entertainers, because dealing with things like per diem can be tricky sometimes. No matter how much or how little you're making, the object is to keep as much of it as possible and diligence about saving receipts is the best way to begin the process.

PART 2

PLAYERS GUIDES

CHAPTER 11

The Touring Guitar Player

Depending on the size of the tour you're on and its budget, you might be lucky enough to have your own guitar tech. Then again, maybe you won't and you'll have to do your own tech work. Let's look at both scenarios.

Be Your Own Tech

Let's say you're on a low-budget tour that can afford only the artist, the band, and a soundperson who does triple duty as the road manager and stage manager. That means you're left to your own devices as far as taking care of your gear. Sure, you did it before when you were playing in local clubs, but now the level is up a notch or two and it's mission critical that your gear works perfectly show after show. How is that accomplished? The best way to avoid any unpleasant gear surprises is to do some simple maintenance before every show. Here's a list of suggestions from a number of notable guitar techs.

- **Make sure that everything is as tight as possible.** This means you have to tighten each screw on your guitars, amps, pedals, and pedalboards, and includes frequently overlooked items like machine heads and the neck-joint screws of Fender guitars. If you use a tube amplifier, make sure that the tubes are secure in their sockets and restrainers and that all the screws on the hardware of the amp and speaker cabinet or baffle board are tight. Be sure to tighten the nut that secures the quarter-inch input and output jacks on all guitars, pedals, and amps. To keep them secure, use this trick: place a single drop of clear nail polish on each screw or nut. They'll stay tight yet it will still be easy enough to break the seal if you need to at a later time. You can also use a thread-locking product like Loctite.

- **Make sure that you have a spare cable available at all times.** Cables are always the first things to fail, since they're constantly plugged in and unplugged, stomped on, dropped, and kicked. Some cables last for years with nary a problem, while others start to crackle soon after purchase. One thing's for sure, they all die sooner or later, so have a backup ready.

Likewise, if you use a wireless unit instead of a cable, have a spare transmitter ready to go. Transmitters are pretty sturdy and reliable, but if you decide to play on your back and it gets crushed, having an extra can save the day. Also have a long cable available in case you can't get rid of some random radio interference or have a frequency-selection problem at a venue.

- **Use DeoxIT D5 on electronic connections like jacks.** DeoxIT (see **Fig. 11.1**) is a space-age contact cleaner that NASA uses on every electrical contact of all its space shuttles to keep them corrosion free. Simple corrosion (or metal oxidation, commonly known as rust) is the number one problem when it comes to metal-on-metal connections like jacks and plugs and relays. Any time a jack crackles, give it a quick shot of DeoxIT, work the plug in and out a few times, and if nothing is wrong with the jack or plug itself, the crackle will disappear like magic. This is especially important even on jacks that you might not often use, like amplifier insert jacks, which can cause the amp to drop in level or change tone at the slightest hint of corrosion. DeoxIT is a high-tech product, yet can still be found at any electronic-parts store like Radio Shack, and even some large drugstores.

Fig. 11.1: A can of DeoxIT D5 contact cleaner.

Fig. 11.2: A Gorgomyte fret-cleaner cloth.

• **Use Gorgomyte for cleaning frets**. When you're under the bright lights, it gets hot and your hands are going to sweat. At worst, this can cause your strings to corrode if your sweat is particularly acidic, or, at least, you'll get a buildup of gunk around the walls of the frets that makes them hard to clean. That's where Gorgomyte comes in (see **Fig. 11.2**). It's a nontoxic, chemically treated polishing cloth developed by guitar tech Jimmy Johnson just for polishing frets and cleaning fingerboards. You'll be surprised how much better the neck will feel. Use it to keep the fingerboard shiny and fresh, and every couple of weeks also use a bit of Dunlop 65 Ultimate Lemon Oil and rub it off with a microfiber cloth. Check out Gorgomyte.com for more information.

• **When you change strings, make sure that the new ones are stretched out sufficiently.** Many techs suggest that you stretch the new string three times: stretch and tune, restretch and retune, and restretch and retune again. That should keep the string from slipping out of tune during the show without it losing its life.

• **Use multiple tuners to be absolutely sure you're in tune.** Most pro techs use a combination of tuners in order to speed up the tuning process and to perform a self-check. Use a traditional LED or meter tuner like a Roland TU-12 to get it in the ballpark, and then fine-tune that with a strobe tuner like one from the Peterson family.

• **Carry plenty of spares**. You have to be prepared for the most common malfunctions, and you can never assume that you'll be lucky enough to be able to get replacements quickly on the road. Being prepared is the best way to keep a simple breakdown from stopping a show.

• **Clean your guitars.** This isn't mission-critical, but it's something that a good tech would do for you on every show. The bright lights are going to show up those smudges and sweat lines like you wouldn't believe. Use a cleaner like Dunlop 65 that's specially designed for modern guitar surfaces.

• **Leave the expensive guitars at home.** This is an especially good idea if you're going to play festivals. There'll be a lot of stagehands around that aren't aware of the value of an instrument (and a few who will know its value all too well), and things can get banged around pretty easily.

The guys in Massive Attack told me they just did a festival in Turkey, where the local stage-hands were 60- and 70-year-old men who were actual sheepherders their whole lives. We're talking about handling delicate instruments, and they're dropping them like it was a rock in a well. —Walter Earl

THE GUITAR PLAYER'S UTILITY KIT

Murphy's Law says that "If something can go wrong, it will go wrong!" so you have to be prepared for anything that might come up while on the road so that you can get back up and running as soon as possible. Things break, but a pro is always ready. The following list of items prepares you for just about anything. Each item should be considered just as essential to bring on tour as your guitar and amp are.

- At least one full set of tubes for each tube amplifier you bring
- A package of fuses for each amp you bring
- At least a box of strings for each guitar (a box has 10 or 12 sets)
- Spare E strings for each gauge of strings
- 2 extra string winders (you can lose these easily)
- 2 digital tuners as described above (with a backup just in case)
- Wire snips
- Needle-nose pliers
- Cable strippers
- A Phillips screwdriver
- A flat-head screwdriver
- A set of Allen wrenches
- A light source (like a flashlight or a clip-on book light from Radio Shack)
- Gaffer's or duct tape
- Superglue
- A cable tester or multimeter
- At least 2 extra 10' instrument cables (1/4" to 1/4")
- At least 2 extra 25' instrument cables (1/4" to 1/4")
- An extra 5' instrument cable
- Extra short cables for connecting effects
- Extra RCA cables or various cable adapters, like 1/4" to RCA,
- RCA to 1/4", and 1/4" to XLR
- An extra AC cable
- An AC extension cable
- An extra power strip
- At least one box of picks
- 2 spare guitar straps
- An extra slide

- An extra capo
- Polish, like Dunlop 65
- Lemon oil
- A microfiber cloth
- DeoxIT
- Gorgomyte fretboard cleaner
- Any special DI if it's part of your sound
- A spare of any pedal that you feel is critical to your sound
- Spare 9V batteries (if you use pedals or have a preamp built into your guitar)
- S pare AA batteries
- Spare power supplies for pedals
- A spare universal 9V wall wart
- A small notepad
- A pen
- A couple of pencils
- A box of Sharpies
- Earplugs

Your Guitar Tech

Chances are good that if you're hitting the road, a bona fide guitar tech will be part of your crew. You might have to share a tech with another player or two, but he's the helping hand you need at this level. Let's take a look at what you can expect from your tech.

WHERE TO FIND A TECH

Most techs, like pretty much all the crew, are found through word of mouth. People who are good at what they do sooner or later begin to work for higher-profile clients, who play on bills or festivals with other high-profile clients, and word gets around. When it comes right down to it, this is a small industry and everyone is connected to everyone else by only a few degrees of separation.

In the event that your first choice or two or three is either unavailable or too much of a hit to the tour budget, there are alternatives. You can try Crewspace.com, which is a private, invitation-only job site for qualified (meaning experienced) touring professionals. Other sites to check out include roadie.net and roadjobs.com.

Something to take note of, there's no certification for a guitar tech, and just because someone has been on the road with a major act before doesn't necessarily mean that he has the chops required for your particular gig. Most techs start out as friends of the band and have little experience beyond that. On the other hand, many techs have a long history of instrument or electronic repair behind them, gaining their experience in the repair shops of music stores before being lured out on the road.

WHAT TO LOOK FOR IN A TECH

The most important quality to look for in a tech is to find someone that you can get along with and trust with your gear. Even if you find someone who is capable, if you can't stand the guy, you won't be happy and he won't be happy either, which can put a lot of strain on everyone cooped up in a bus for six weeks.

You also want someone who shares your musical sensibilities. You can't always expect someone who doesn't care much about the type of music you're playing to relate to some of the problems you might have performing, or to the wear and tear or specific types of maintenance your gear requires.

While you really need someone with enough experience to do the job, using someone who'd rather take your place onstage than be a tech can also be hazardous to the show and your mental well-being. Here's an anonymous story from an excellent tech.

A European band goes to tour the States and is told that there'll be a guitar tech for them. This guitar tech is a musician that is starting to promote his own band. He posts on his personal website that he'll be touring with this European band "not to play with them, just to give them a hand" (he was being paid). The results?

The guitar players always had to tune their own guitars onstage at the beginning of almost every show if they wanted to play tuned.

Important gear was lost, like leather guitar straps, screws from guitar parts, and (this is amazing) [there was] a completely broken truss rod from a 5-string, very good bass guitar. When I received this guitar to try and fix it, I simply couldn't believe it and showed it to another luthier, who was astonished as well. Good thing the endorsement solved the problem by providing a new instrument.

Here's another little story from an anonymous guitar tech about what can happen if you hire an unqualified tech.

A band brings a technician to tour with them in Europe. [There was] only one guitar (that had to be restringed [sic] everyday) and one bass guitar to take care [of]. On the third or fourth show I saw this:

During changeover, he wasn't at all at ease with anything there. We could see that he had a funny way of handling cabinets and amplifiers, the way he misplaced microphones, and just generally showed a total lack of experience.

The gig starts, and the guy didn't know where to be positioned onstage (space was not much of a problem), and the tour manager had to point him to the place where he should be. Not long after, the guitar player calls him over (he was really pissed off) and tells him, "The volume should be on 7 and it was on 3! How could you not hear that during line-check?"

By the fourth or fifth song, one guitar string breaks, [and] the musician leaves the guitar by the amp and cab and leaves the stage. The tech, instead of taking the guitar, runs after the musician and asks, "What should I do?" The answer: "Put me to play!" The guy: "But I have no strings. I forgot them on the bus. That's why I didn't restring the guitar today" (the bus was only a few hundred feet away from the venue, and I saw this guy spending the whole afternoon in the dressing room on his laptop). Musician: "I don't care, put me to play. Borrow a guitar, ask for strings, whatever . . ."

Then some guys from one of the guest bands arrived, and knowing what was going on, gave him a bunch of guitar strings for him to work it out. Then he asked the TM [tour manager] to bring him his plumberlike toolbox, and said, "OK, I'll do this in two seconds," with the guitar on his lap, sitting on the stairway.

After some continuous instructions from the guitar player about microtuning and the nut lock that apparently he didn't know about, and a lot of shaking while trying first to replace the string correctly and then to tune it, some ten minutes have passed and the rest of the band is still onstage waiting. He finally shouts out in a high-pitched crying voice, "Oh my god! I can't tune it!"

Then the player just grabbed the guitar and went onstage saying, "Enough, I'll do it myself," and did it on his stage tuner. The show carried on while the guy was still saying, "Wait, wait, it's not locked." I seriously believe that this guy was paying the band loads of money to let him screw up that big."

So be careful who you hire. Make sure you get references and that you follow them up. And make sure you feel comfortable with the guy before having him sign on. After all, he'll be continuously handling many of the things that are the most dear to you. For more insight into the world of a guitar tech, check out the interview with Michael McConnell in part 3 of this book.

THE TECH'S RESPONSIBILITIES

Most guitar techs are responsible for taking care of your guitars, amps, and pedals, the exception being a celebrity guitar player who may employ a separate tech for just his guitars and another for his electronics. That doesn't happen that often, so for the purpose of this discussion we'll assume that the guitar tech is looking after the guitarist's entire rig. Here's what you can expect from a tech.

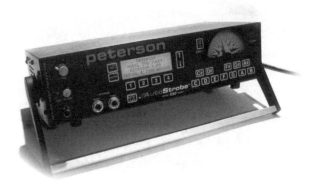
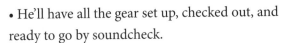

Fig. 11.3: A Peterson model 590 strobe tuner.

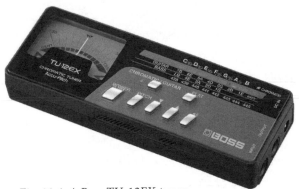

Fig. 11.4: A Boss TU-12EX tuner.

Fig. 11.5: A typical guitar vault.

• He'll have all the gear set up, checked out, and ready to go by soundcheck.

• He'll have each guitar cleaned of all grease, dirt, and fingerprints.

• He'll make sure the strings are changed as needed and that the action and intonation have been checked on every guitar. Many players require a string change on all their guitars before every show because either they like the sound of new strings or the strings become corroded from the acid in their fingers. Other players feel it's okay to go a few gigs between changes, and yet others change their strings according to the number of songs played (for instance, after eight songs). Yet others want their strings changed only when a string is broken. Whenever the strings are changed, the tech makes sure they're properly stretched so they stay in tune.

• For tuning, most techs don't rely on just a single tuner, and double-check everything with a second tuner just to be sure that the guitar's in tune. Usually a strobe tuner like the Peterson 590 (see **Fig. 11.3**) or their StroboSoft software tuning package is used, backed up with a more low-tech tuner like a Korg DTR-2000 or DTR-1 or a Boss TU-12 (see Fig. **11.4**).

• After each guitar is used, the guitar tech cleans the strings with a cloth and places it on a stand or guitar vault (see **Fig. 11.5**).

• He'll make sure that all amps and pedals are in working order, and that all cables and wireless systems work flawlessly.

- Before each show, he'll replace the batteries in the wireless transmitter and in any pedals or guitars that may require a fresh one.
- During the show, the tech is always alert to the playing status of the guitar player, and is ready to replace a guitar if a string breaks or provide a workaround for a piece of gear that malfunctions.

Fig. 11.6: Extra picks on an amp.

- The tech is also responsible for handing the appropriate guitar to the player as each song requires, and making sure that any wireless gear is operating and has the right broadcast channel selected on the new guitar.
- The tech always makes sure that enough picks are available, either laid out on top of an amplifier or taped to a mic stand with double-sided tape, and may hand the player a towel or beverage during the show (see **Fig. 11.6**).
- Techs may be involved in the guitar player's performance during a show, actively switching effects on and off at various points in the songs, so that the player doesn't have to think about it.
- The tech tears down the rig immediately after the show. Most band gear is always packed on the truck first, so everything has to be packed and on the truck within about 45 minutes after the last notes of the last song.

THE TECH'S TOOLBOX

Besides the spares listed in "The Guitar Player's Utility Kit" sidebar above), many guitar techs also bring along the following items:

- A soldering iron
- Solder
- Machine heads
- Nuts
- Volume pots
- Tone pots
- Spare pickups
- Pickup surrounds
- Volume knobs for guitars, amps, and pedals
- Bridges
- Tail pieces
- Strap buttons

- Fret wire
- Fret files
- Nut files
- A variety of screws, washers, and nuts
- Steel wool
- A power drill
- A router
- Wet and dry sandpaper
- A bench vice
- Spray glue
- Other guitar tuners
- A small amplifier for tuning

COMMUNICATING WITH YOUR TECH

Most players and techs work out a series of head or hand signals so that the player can indicate to the tech exactly he needs during the show. Likewise, the tech sometimes has to get the attention of the player, so he may rig a small indicator light with a red filter over it (so it doesn't interfere with the stage lighting) and place it where the player will see it easily. Do you need an amp turned up? More gain or distortion? Another guitar? A towel? These should all be worked out beforehand to keep both the player and the tech from getting frustrated.

Be very clear about what you want from the tech. For instance, if you just say, "More echo," does that mean you need more repeats, or does it mean you want a louder echo volume? If you say, "Louder," what does that mean exactly? Should the guitar amp be turned up onstage, or in the monitors? Should the effects be louder? It's easy to misinterpret a short statement, so you have to be as specific as possible to get precisely what you need in the shortest time period.

A Word About Gear

Touring is completely different from playing on the weekends in your local clubs or recording in your own or someone else's studio. Reliability is the key, even at the sake of having to slightly sacrifice getting the perfect sound (although hopefully you can achieve both).

KEEPING YOUR AMPS RELIABLE

Many techs will recommend that you keep your rig as simple as possible, because then there's less to go wrong. If something does malfunction, it is easier to diagnose and faster to fix with a simple rig. Hot-rodded and jury-rigged systems can also cause problems, because boutique goes hand in hand with fragile and temperamental.

Fig. 11.7: Pete Townshend's backup amp.

That being said, it's now standard for every guitar player to travel with a backup amplifier (although on a low-budget tour, there may be only one backup for all the players). Tube amplifiers have a habit of malfunctioning at the most inopportune times, so if there's an amp that's important to your sound, a second one should be considered a necessity (see **Fig. 11.7**). Keep it onstage, turned on, and ready to go at a moment's notice.

Many players (Tommy Shaw of Styx, for one, and Phil Collen of Def Leppard, for another) have eliminated speaker cabinets from their rigs altogether by using a Palmer PDI-03 speaker simulator (see **Fig. 11.8**). With floor monitors and in-ear systems being so sophisticated these days, being able to hear yourself is no longer the issue it once was. If you can get the sound you need with your amp off-stage or going direct to the FOH and monitor consoles through a simulator, your FOH and monitor engineers will love

Fig. 11.8: A Palmer PDI-03 speaker simulator.

you, since it will make their jobs a lot easier.

One thing that bugs guitar players the most is how the sound of their amps can change from venue to venue. This is usually caused by poorly regulated power that fluctuates from anywhere between 95 and 120 volts. One of the most valuable and useful pieces of gear is a transformer-based power-regulator system like the Furman AR-20 (see **Fig. 11.9**) to keep the voltage steady. Whether the power is being provided from an outside generator or a fluctuating power grid, you can be sure that the voltage

Fig. 11.9: A Furman
AR-20 power regulator.

and your sound will remain the same for every show.

If you're lucky enough to get to tour with an elite act doing gigs all over the world, you may be required to have more than one rig available. It's not uncommon for players in these situations to have as many as many as three entire rigs. An "A" rig might be used in the States while a "B" rig is in transit to Europe or Asia in an economical manner to save on shipping costs. In some cases, there might even be a smaller "C" rig that's scaled down for small venues or television shows.

PEDALBOARDS

While some players may still be purists, preferring just a guitar, a cable, and an amp, most guitar players now have an assortment of pedals to help them get their sound. A haphazard pedal setup is a recipe for disaster on the road, so some organization and repeatability is necessary, hence the need for a pedalboard.

Fig. 11.10: The Edge's
pedalboard.

Many pedalboards are nothing more than a piece of plywood with effects pedals and maybe a power supply connected to it, while others are sophisticated switching systems capable of great complexity. Since artists often demand that the exact sounds of their records be replicated, and those sounds can change quickly from song to song or even within a song, more and more guitar players are acquiring pedalboards that have the ability to set up presets. These are made by companies like TC Electronic (the G System) and Custom Audio Electronics, among others.

Bob Bradshaw's Custom Audio Electronics is the pioneer in pedalboards and is still in the forefront of pedalboard technology, having branched into preamps, amplifiers, smaller switching systems, and even effects pedals. Many superstars such as The Edge (see **Fig. 11.10** to see his pedalboard), Steve Lukather, Eddie Van Halen, and Billy Joe Armstrong have custom-made CAE pedalboards as the centerpiece of their live rigs.

Obviously, you may not have the financial resources of a superstar player, but a pedalboard of some sort may be in your future, if the songs of an artist you're touring with demand it.

CHAPTER 12

The Touring Bass Player

It used to be that a bass player would show up at a gig (even a touring gig) with just a bass and an amp, and while some still employ such a simple setup, many of today's touring bass players have rigs that are sophisticated enough to require their own tech. This is all the more reason to be prepared for any eventuality, regardless of whether you have a tech. Here are some things to consider.

Be Your Own Tech

In the event that your tour can't afford a dedicated bass tech, you may be forced to do at least some of your own teching. (You can refer to the section on self-teching in chapter 11, since just about everything is the same for bass as it is for guitar.)

THE BASS PLAYER'S UTILITY KIT

You know that something on your rig will break sooner or later. It always does, especially at the worst time. You can't avoid a visit from Mr. Murphy, but at least you can be ready for him. The following list of items prepares you for just about anything. Each item should be considered just as essential to playing a session as your bass and amp.

- 2 spare power tubes
- 2 spare 12AX7 preamp tubes
- Spares for any other tube in the amp (especially important for hard-to-find tubes in Ampeg SVT heads)
- A package of fuses for each amp
- At least a couple sets of strings for each bass (more if you change your strings often)
- 2 different digital tuners (with a backup just in case)
- Wire snips
- Needle-nose pliers
- Cable strippers
- A Phillips screwdriver
- A flat-head screwdriver
- A set of Allen wrenches
- A light source (like a flashlight or a clip-on book light from Radio Shack)
- Gaffer's or duct tape
- Superglue
- A cable tester or multimeter
- At least 2 extra 10' instrument cables (1/4" to 1/4")
- At least 2 extra 25' instrument cables (1/4" to 1/4")
- An extra 5' instrument cable
- Extra short cables for connecting effects
- Extra RCA cables or various cable adapters like 1/4" to RCA,
- RCA to 1/4", and 1/4" to XLR
- An extra AC cable
- An AC extension cable
- An extra power strip
- At least one box of picks
- 2 spare guitar straps
- Polish, like Dunlop 65
- Lemon oil

- A microfiber cloth
- DeoxIT
- Gorgomyte fretboard cleaner
- Any special DI if it's part of your sound
- A spare of any pedal that you feel is critical to your sound
- Spare 9V batteries (if you use pedals or have a preamp built into your bass)
- Spare AA batteries
- Spare power supplies for pedals
- A spare universal 9V wall wart
- A small notepad
- A pen
- A couple of pencils
- A box of Sharpies
- Earplugs

Your Bass Tech

The tech requirements of a bass player are different from those of a guitar player even though they both play string instruments, and a tech has to be aware of those nuances. Many modern players use a variety of pedals, multiple electric basses in different tunings, upright or acoustic bass, a modular amplifier rig, and even keyboard or bass pedals. These diverse usages require that a tech have a wide variety of skills and talents.

WHERE TO FIND A TECH

Most techs are found through word of mouth, since the industry is smaller than you think and everyone seems to be connected to everyone else by only a few degrees of separation. Ask around and be specific about your requirements. Tour managers are always a good source for getting a few names, as are other bass and guitar players. Other techs are also a great source for referrals.

In the event that you can't find anyone suitable that fits in your budget, you have alternatives. Try Crewspace.com, which is a private, invitation-only job site for qualified (meaning experienced) touring professionals, or check out other similar sites, like roadie.net and roadjobs.com.

Just remember, get references and follow up on them. You don't want someone handling your gear who's unqualified or, even worse, incompetent. If you want a couple of horror stories to scare you straight, check out the section "What to Look for in a Tech" in chapter 11.

THE TECH'S RESPONSIBILITIES

Unlike some guitar techs who specialize in only guitars and never deal with amps and electronics, most bass techs are in charge of the entire bass rig, regardless of its sophistication. Here's what you can expect from a tech.

- He'll have all the gear set up, checked out, and ready to go by soundcheck.
- He'll have each bass cleaned of all grease, dirt, and fingerprints.
- He'll make sure the strings are changed as needed and that the action and intonation have been checked on every bass. For some players, that means the strings are changed only when they break, while others want them changed before every show. As with guitar tuning, most bass techs don't rely on just a single tuner, and instead double-check everything with a second tuner like a strobe tuner like one from the Peterson family of products (see **Fig. 11.3** in chapter 11).
- After each bass is used, the bass tech cleans the strings with a cloth and places the instrument on a stand or in a vault.
- He'll make sure that all amps and pedals are in working order, and that all cables and wireless systems work flawlessly.
- Before each show, he'll replace the batteries in the wireless transmitter and any pedals or basses or other instruments that the bass player might play during the show.
- During the show, the tech is alert to the playing status of the bass player, always ready to replace a bass if a string breaks or to find a workaround if a piece of gear malfunctions.
- The tech is also responsible for handing the appropriate bass to the player as each song requires (like an acoustic or a 5-string), and making sure that any wireless gear is operating and has the right broadcast channel selected on the new instrument.
- The tech makes sure that enough picks are available (if they're being used by the bass player), and either lays them out on top of an amplifier or tapes them to a mic stand with double-sided tape, and he may hand the player a towel or a beverage during the show.
- Techs may also be involved in the bass player's performance during a show, actively switching effects on and off at various points in the songs, so that the player doesn't have to think about doing it.
- Finally, the bass tech tears down the rig immediately after the show. Most

band gear is always packed on the truck first, so everything has to be packed and on the truck within about 45 minutes after the last notes of the last song.

COMMUNICATING WITH YOUR TECH

Most players and techs work out a series of head or hand signals, so that the player can indicate to the tech exactly he needs during the show. Likewise, the tech sometimes has to get the attention of the player, so a small indicator light with a red filter over it (so it doesn't interfere with the stage lighting) is sometimes placed where the player will see it easily. Do you need an amp turned up? More gain or distortion? Another bass? A towel? These should all be worked out beforehand to keep both the player and the tech from getting frustrated because of poor communication.

A Word About Gear

Touring is completely different from playing on the weekends in your local club or recording in your own or someone else's studio. Reliability is the key, even at the sake of having to slightly sacrifice getting the perfect sound (although hopefully, you can achieve both). Bass amps take a beating because of the low-frequency vibrations that are integral to their functioning, and that requires taking extra precautions.

KEEP YOUR AMPS RELIABLE

It's pretty standard these days for every bass player to travel with a backup amplifier head, no matter how reliable the main one seems to be. Tube amplifiers have a habit of malfunctioning at the most inopportune times, and a solid-state amp's circuitry is intricate enough that it may have to be sent to the factory for repair. That's why if there's an amp that's important to your sound, a second one should be considered a necessity. Keep it onstage, turned on, and ready to go at a moment's notice.

One thing that bugs both guitar and bass players the most is how the sound of their amps can change from venue to venue. This is usually caused by poorly regulated power that fluctuates from anywhere between 95 and 120 volts. One of the most valuable and useful pieces of gear is a transformer-based power-regulator system, like the Furman AR-20 (see **Fig. 11.9** in chapter 11) to keep the voltage steady. Whether the power is being provided from an outside generator or a fluctuating power grid, you can be sure that the voltage and your sound will remain the same for every show. See if you can get the tour to buy a large one that can be used for the entire backline.

CHAPTER 13

The Touring Drummer

Regardless of the size of the budget, the drummer is normally the first one on the tour to get a tech. Why? Not so much because of the normal maintenance of drums, which is substantial, but because of the physical nature of drumming. The last thing a drummer wants to do at the end of the show is pack up his kit. That being said, you might be on a low-budget tour that just doesn't have enough dough to hire someone, and you'll have to do your own tech work. Let's look at both scenarios.

Be Your Own Tech

You were your own tech for all those years you played in local clubs and never thought too much about it, but when you're touring everything is different. You have to be absolutely sure that your kit doesn't let you down in the middle of a show and you have a plan for any contingencies. How do you do that? Simple and constant maintenance before every show does more to keep your drums from experiencing a serious breakdown than anything else. Here's a list of suggestions from a number of notable drum techs.

- Change the heads regularly. On bigger tours, some drummers change their heads for every show. Some do it on a schedule, such as every two shows for toms and snare and every five for the kick. Whatever your schedule might be, be sure to stick with it to make sure that your drums sound their best and to avoid having a problem during the show.

Fig. 13.1: A custom drum flight case.

• Stretch the heads evenly, so the head doesn't warp. Bring them up to tension as evenly as possible, then loosen the tension back down a bit to let them settle, then bring it back up to the tuning you want.

• Soft cases placed on the drums before they're placed into flight cases will help prevent them from having thermal shock. If you're touring in cold places, shells that are taken out of the truck cold and then placed directly into the warmth of the venue can warp. You can also buy road cases especially made for providing greater protection against extreme heat and cold (see **Fig. 13.1**).

• Use Loctite on bottom heads that don't need tuning that often. Loctite is a thread-locking fluid that can be used as a replacement for less reliable washers (see **Fig. 13.2**). Since bottom heads aren't changed as often, a little Loctite can help them keep their tuning.

• Check every screw on each piece of your hardware and tighten anything that's loose. Doing just this one thing can save you a lot of heartache later.

• Use an electric drill to change heads quickly. This works very well, especially when taking the heads off the drum. Be careful not to overtorque anything as you put the new heads on.

Fig. 13.2: Loctite thread-locking fluid.

• Have a rug that's marked with the location of where your stands and drums should be placed. This will help to make sure that your kit is set up consistently every night, and will make it easier for someone to help you if you're in a hurry.

• Consider Drumplates (drumplates.com) to hold your hardware in place. Every drummer's constant gripe is about hardware moving during a performance. Drumplates place a moveable barrier on a hard plastic plate to keep everything from moving (see **Fig. 13.3**). It will not only keep your kit solid, but will also make it sound better.

• Keep everything clean. Drums look bad under the lights when they're dirty and have fingerprint smudges all over them. Put your drums in the best light and clean them.

• Cymbals that are bright and shiny may look better, but they last longer if they're not cleaned. Use some warm

Fig. 13.3: Drumplates

soapy water to get the dirt out of the grooves. If you really want them shiny, use a solution of two-thirds Windex to one-third ammonia.

TUNING THE DRUMS

Many drummers don't know enough about why their kit sounds the way it does, and unfortunately, that applies to drum tuning as well. All drummers are taught the basics of drum tuning sometime during their education, but knowing how to do it and knowing what to listen for are two different things. Here are some tips from Ross Garfield, the famous Drum Doctor (drumdoctors.com), to get you started.

Prepping the Drums for New Heads

In order for drums to sound their best, the edges of the drum shell have to be cut properly, and this is something that no one ever checks, or even thinks of checking, until it's time to change the heads. When you take the heads off, all the edges of the shell should lie exactly flat against a flat surface. I'll put the shell on a piece of glass or granite and shine a light over the top of the shell, then I'll get down to where the edge of the drum hits the granite. If I see a light at any point, that means there's a low spot on the edge of the shell and the drum will be hard to tune and probably have some funny overtones. So the first thing to do is make sure that your drum shells are "true" (the edges are even all around the drum) The next thing is for your shell edge to have a bevel to it, and not be flat on the bottom, because again, this can make the drum difficult to tune and have some undesirable overtones.

If you have either of these problems with a drum, send it back to the manufacturer. Don't try to cut the edges of your drum shells yourself, since it doesn't cost that much money for the manufacture to do it and it should be done by someone who knows exactly what they're doing. Once your drum shells are in good shape, then tuning is a lot easier.

New Heads

The first thing I'll do when tuning my drums is put a fresh set of top and bottom heads on them. Nine times out of ten, I'll put white Remo Ambassadors on the tops, clear Remo Ambassadors on the bottoms, and a Remo clear Powerstroke 3 on the kick drum. I'll use a white Ambassador or a coated black dot Ambassador on the snare top and either a clear Diplomat or a coated Ambassador on the bottom.

A lot of your decision about what type of head to use depends on how deep the drum is. If it's five inches or less, I usually go with an

Ambassador; if it's six and one-half inches or larger, I'll usually go with a Diplomat. Having just this little bit of information can make a real difference in how the kit sounds.

A heavy hitter will get more low end out of a drum that's tuned higher just because of the way he hits, so I usually tune a drum a little tighter if the drummer is a heavy hitter. I might move into different heads as well, like an Emperor or something thicker.

I just kind of move the combination of drumheads around to get different things. If I want a heavier sound, I'll use a thicker head. If I want it brighter with more attack, I'll use a thinner head. I usually don't go any thinner than an Ambassador, and I usually don't go any thicker than an Emperor. —Ricky Lawson, a drummer for Michael Jackson, Eric Clapton, Steely Dan, among many others

The Tuning Technique

Many drummers don't know the proper way to tune their drums, but it's really not that hard. For a proper tune job, you've got to keep all of the tension rods even, so that they have the same tension at each lug.

You hit the head an inch in front of the lug, and if you do it enough times, you'll hear which ones are higher and which are lower. Your goal is for the pitch to sound the same at each lug. When the pitch (the tension) is the same at each lug, then when you hit the drum in the center you should have a nice even decay.

TIP: Some drummers and techs feel that they get a truer note by using a mallet instead of a stick for tuning.

Tune the top and the bottom head to the same pitch at first, then take the bottom head down a third to a fifth below the top head.

There's a lot of different theories about how a drum should sound, but the one that works best for me is when the top head is not exactly the same pitch as the bottom. I tune the top head about a minor third above the bottom head, when you're just barely tapping it right on the edge near the lug. —Bernie Dresel, formerly of the Brian Setzer Orchestra

I tap the side of the shell to see how it will sound in the room, then I tune it accordingly so that the drum is working at its maximum value in relation to the room. I do that everywhere I go, whether it's a ballroom or a wedding or Studio D at Village Recorders or Conway [a famous Hollywood recording studio] or The House of Blues or the Gibson Amphitheater. I always tune the drums for the room. My idea of a good-sounding drum is when you can just throw a mic in front of it and it works without any EQ or processing, which engineers love. —Johnny "Vatos" Hernandez, Los Angeles session drummer, formerly of Oingo Boingo

Snare Drum Tuning Tips

The snare is the most important drum in the set. It's the voice of the song, since you hear it on at least every 2 and 4, so it's important to get the snare tuned to where you want it first. I like the ring of the drum to decay with the snares.

If the snare drum has too much ring:
- Tune the heads lower.
- Use a heavier head, like a coated CS with the dot on the bottom or a coated Emperor.
- Use a full or partial muffling ring.
- Have the edges checked and/or recut to a flatter angle.

If the snare drum doesn't have enough ring:
- Tune the head higher.
- Use a thinner head, like a coated Ambassador or Diplomat.
- Have the edges checked and/or recut to a sharper angle.

If the snares buzz when the tom-toms are hit:
- Check that the snares are straight. Replace as needed.
- Check that the snares are flat and centered on the drum.
- Loosen the bottom head.
- Retune the offending toms.
- Use an alternate snare drum.

I don't think it's good to tune the snare drum on the snare stand. It's better on a table or floor, so it's laying flat. You make sure you get your head on flat if you have to change one, then tighten each lug so that it's barely touching the rim, then just finger-tighten the lugs (crisscrossing as you go) so you make sure that you don't overtighten one. Then you can start using the drum key. —Bernie Dresel

Tuning the Kick Drum

If the kick drum isn't punchy and lacks power when played in the context of the music, try the following:

- Try increasing and decreasing the amount of muffling in the drum, or try a different blanket or pillow.
- Change to a heavier, uncoated head, like a clear Emperor or Powerstroke 3.
- Change to a thinner front head or one with a larger cutout.
- Have the edges recut to create more attack.

Tuning the Toms

- The kick and snare are the two most important drums, and I tune the toms around them to make sure that the rack toms aren't being set off by the snare.
- I like the toms to have a nice even decay. Usually I'll tune the drums so that the smallest drums have the shortest decay, with the decay getting longer as the drums get bigger.
- I tune each tom as far apart as the song will permit. It's easy to get the right spread between a 13- and a 16-inch tom, but it's more difficult to get it between a 12 and a 13. I try to tune the 12 up and the 13 down a little.

If any of the tom-toms are difficult to tune, don't blend together, or have an unwanted "growl", try the following:

- Check the top heads for dents and replace as necessary.
- Check the evenness of tension all around on the top and bottom heads.
- Tighten the bottom head.
- Have the bearing edges checked and recut as required.

If the floor tom has an undesirable "basketball-type" after-ring, try this:

- Loosen the bottom head.
- Check the top heads for dents and replace as necessary.
- Loosen the top head.
- Switch to a different type or weight of top or bottom head, like a clear • Ambassador or an Emperor.
- Have the bearing edges recut to emphasize the lower partials.

So what I try to do between my three toms—the 12", 14", and 16"—is to have them maybe a fourth apart in pitch, and that way you don't get an octave between the highest tom and the lowest and they sound musical together. Now if you have a lot of toms, then maybe tuning them a major third apart could work, but with three toms I think a fourth is good because all three are tuned within the same octave and a fifth is too much because then they're not. —Bernie Dresel

Cymbals

Thicker cymbals are made more with a live situation in mind, as they're made to be loud and to cut through the band. Thinner cymbals, on the other hand, sound better for recording. No matter which you prefer, it's best to keep all of your cymbals about the same weight so that the level between them will remain even. Not only will this sound better, but it will help your FOH engineer get the best balance on your drums.

If the cymbals are cracking or breaking with greater frequency, try the following:
- Always transport the cymbals in a top-quality, reinforced cymbal case or bag to avoid their getting nicks that can become cracks.
- Use the proper cymbal felts, washers, and sleeves at all times.
- Avoid overtightening the cymbal stand.
- Use larger or heavier cymbals that you won't have to overplay to hear.

THE DRUMMER'S UTILITY KIT

Here's a list of items that can prepare you for just about anything Murphy can throw at you. Each item should be considered just as essential to playing a show as your kit is.

- Spare snare heads
- Spare kick drum heads
- Spare snare strainers
- A spare strainer cord
- A spare kick drum pedal
- Spare kick drum springs
- A few impact pads
- Head-dampening material like Moongel
- Spare tension rods
- A spare kick drum beater
- A spare snare stand
- A spare hi-hat stand

- A spare hi-hat clutch
- A spare snare drum
- Wing nuts
- Washers
- Spare cymbal sleeves
- Spare cymbal felts
- Lots of drum keys
- Lots of sticks
- Mallets
- Wire snips
- needle-nose pliers
- A Phillips screwdriver
- A flat-head screwdriver
- A speed wrench
- A pocketknife
- A set of Allen wrenches
- A small hammer
- Lithium grease
- Small rags or microfiber towels
- A light source (like a flashlight or a clip-on book light)
- Duct tape
- Superglue
- A feather duster (to reach dirt in hard to reach places)
- Furniture polish (to wipe fingerprints off)

If you provide your own click or use electronic pads or triggers, also bring the following:
- At least as many extra instrument cables as you're using
- At least an extra ¼"-to-XLR cable
- A set of headphones
- Spare 9V batteries
- Spare AA batteries
- A spare universal 9V wall wart
- A small notepad
- A pen
- 2 pencils
- A magic marker
- Band-Aids
- A towel
- Earplugs

Your Drum Tech

The chances are good that if you're hitting the road, you're going to have a drum tech be part of your crew. Here's what you need to know about your right-hand man.

WHERE TO FIND A TECH

As stated in this section in the previous chapters, most techs are found through word of mouth. People that are good at what they do begin to make a mark, and word gets around sooner or later. When it comes right down to it, this industry is small and everyone is connected to everyone else by only a few degrees of separation.

In the event that your first choice or two or three is either unavailable or too much of a hit to the tour budget, there are alternatives. You can try Crewspace.com, which is a private, invitation-only job site for qualified (meaning experienced) touring professionals. Other sites include roadie. net and roadjobs.com.

WHAT TO LOOK FOR IN A TECH

Perhaps the important qualities of a tech are that they are someone that you like and can get along with and that you can trust with your gear. Even if the guy is capable, you won't be a happy camper if you dislike him and he won't be happy, either, which is not a great working environment for either of you.

Next, you want someone who shares the same musical sensibilities that you have. You can't always expect someone who doesn't care much about the type of music you're playing to relate to some of the problems you might have performing, or to the wear and tear or specific types of maintenance your gear requires.

Finally, you want someone who can play a little, so he can fill in for you during soundcheck if necessary, but who isn't a frustrated player that would rather take your job than help you do yours. Really good techs know their place, so this is rarely a problem, but if someone seems too inexpensive or available, this could be the reason.

THE TECH'S RESPONSIBILITIES

Depending on his experience and knowledge, a drum tech can help you with a lot more than the obvious drum setup and maintenance. That being said, here's what you can expect from a tech.

- He'll have your entire kit set up, checked out, and ready to go by soundcheck. This might include only the drums, but it could also include anything that goes on the drum riser, such as microphones and lights.
- He'll have the drums cleaned of all dirt and fingerprints.
- He'll have the heads changed as the schedule requires, and the tuning will be at least in the general ballpark for you to tweak.
- He'll replace the batteries in any wireless units for mics or in-ear monitors that you might use.
- During the show, the tech is alert to the playing status of the drummer, always ready to replace a head or a pedal if one breaks, or to hand you a new stick if you drop one.
- He may also run any electronics for the drummer during the show, like metronomes, clicks, or loops, or he might change programs on electronic drums.
- He may monitor the in-ears or the monitor mix of the drummer and communicate with the monitor mixer the wishes of the drummer.
- In the event of a performance in the round, he may spin the drum riser around as needed.
- He'll tear down the rig immediately after the show. Most band gear is always packed on the truck first, so everything has to be packed and on the truck within about 45 minutes after the last notes of the last song have been played.

THE TECH'S TOOLBOX

Besides the spares listed in "The Drummer's Utility Kit" sidebar above, many drum techs will also bring the following items:

- Woodworking tools
- Clamps
- Wood glue
- Spray adhesive
- Wood screws
- Black cloth to cover up the drums on stage
- Spare pedals
- Tension bolts
- Allen bolts
- Spare cymbals
- A spare kick drum
- Spare cymbal stands
- A spare snare stand

COMMUNICATING WITH YOUR TECH

Most players and techs work out a series of head or hand signals, so that the player can indicate to the tech exactly what he or she needs during the show. Likewise, the tech sometimes has to get the attention of the player, so many put a small indicator light with a red filter over it (so it doesn't interfere with the stage lighting) in a place where the player will see it easily. These ways of communicating should all be worked out before the show, to keep both the player and tech from getting frustrated by lack of communication.

Also, be very clear about what you want from the tech. For instance, if you just say, "More me," does that mean more drums in the mix or more vocals (if the drummer sings)? If you say, "Louder," what does that mean exactly? Should the kick drum be turned up in the monitor mix? Are you referring to the snare? More of the rest of the band? It's easy to misinterpret a short statement, so you have to be as specific as possible to get exactly what you need in the shortest amount of time.

For more information about the world of the drum tech, check out Walter Earl's interview in part III.

CHAPTER 14

The Touring Vocalist

The touring vocalist doesn't need a tech, lots of time to set up, or any particular special treatment. He or she needs only to hear him or herself sufficiently well onstage and to have a way of keeping their voice from being ravaged by the rigors of the road. The road can be especially tough on some singers who aren't able to rest well, but yet others thrive on the steady work and get stronger as the tour goes along. Regardless of which category you fall in to, here are some tips to keep you in great voice each and every night.

Take Care of Yourself

Since the vocalist is the only musician who can't put their instrument away in a protective case after the show, it's important to take good care of it. Eventually, every singer has some vocal trouble, and if you aren't careful, it can lead to long-term damage. That's why it's vital that a singer learn to take care of him or herself.

Aside from being sick, the number one cause of vocal problems is lack of enough sleep. When you're tired, all the parts of your body needed to support your vocal cords can weaken; this leads to improper breathing, and thus throat problems, shortly after you begin singing. Get as much sleep as you can (preferably seven or eight hours) the night before a show, or take a brief nap on the day of the gig so you can feel somewhat refreshed. Since most people don't sleep well on the road, the only way to compensate is to sleep even more than normal.

Avoid consuming milk (and all other dairy products) beginning three to six hours before you sing. Anything with milk in it will cause an excess production of phlegm around your vocal chords, so that's a definite no-no. The old remedy of milk and honey for a rough throat can be soothing after the show, but not before!

Try not to eat within an hour before your performance in order to avoid that excess phlegm again. If you're hungry before a show, don't be afraid to eat, but just eat until you're satisfied and don't stuff yourself with a seven-course meal. If you do feel phlegmy, you'll have the strongest temptation to clear your throat (which can be harmful) immediately after eating, but try to resist the urge for about an hour until you have enough time for your meal to settle and the phlegm to subside.

If you must clear your throat, try to do so without irritating it. Some people say that you should never try to clear your throat, because it can cause irritation or even damage, but doing so is usually necessary because excess mucous really inhibits your singing. The best way to clear your throat is to do a gentle "whispered cough," and then swallow and repeat. If this doesn't work, you need to deal with the excess mucous production. Squeeze a quarter of a lemon into a tall glass of water and sip over a period of about 20 minutes. This should cut through a lot of the excess mucous.

Avoid alcohol, tea (despite popular belief), coffee, cola, and anything else with caffeine. They have a dehydrating effect, which is the opposite of what you need.

Stay hydrated. Drink lots and lots of water (ideally two to three quarts a day—the more the better), because a dry throat can lead to a sore throat. If you're touring through an arid climate like the Pacific Southwest, you might try to warm up your voice in the shower, since the moisture can be an incredible help to your voice. Also, learn to breathe in through your nose as much as possible. This will help moisten the air you breathe in before it reaches your vocal cords.

Finally, some singers swear by Entertainer's Secret (see **Fig. 14.1**), a spray mixture (developed by an ear, nose, and throat specialist) that lubricates the vocal cords. You can get more information about it at www. entertainers-secret.com.

If I'm on a tour that's very vocally demanding, I'll warm up early in the day and then again right before the show. I have a warm-up exercise that I do that I got from a voice teacher in L.A, called Roger Love. Other than that, I don't smoke, and I drink lots of water. Smoking's like the worse thing that you can do for your voice. I also try to make sure that I get enough sleep. If you're a singer, your body is your instrument, so it has to stay rested. —Paul Mirkovich

IF YOU GET A SORE THROAT

Maybe you have a sore throat from a cold or maybe you just sang a bit too hard last night. In any event, you have to be ready to sing again for the show tonight, so you're going to have to take some precautions to be able to get through the gig.

Here are some things to try as soon as you feel yourself getting sore.

Fig. 14.1: Entertainer's Secret throat spray.

• Use your voice as little as possible until it's absolutely necessary. That includes speaking and singing.

• Stay out of the air conditioning. It dries you out, which is the opposite of what you need. If you must be in an air-conditioned room or vehicle, try to speak as little as possible while you're there.

• Drink warm drinks, since they act as decongestants. Fruit drinks that aren't too acidic work best.

• Try this little mixture to make your voice feel better: Squeeze one fresh lemon into a glass, and add in a couple of teaspoons of clear honey and a little bit of water. Gargle, then swallow. The honey coats the vocal chords, and the lemon makes you salivate, thus stopping them from drying out.

• Another remedy you can use to help alleviate a sore throat (and other cold symptoms) is to make some hot water, and then add a mixture of honey and apple cider vinegar. Alone, the vinegar would probably hurt the throat because of its acidic nature, but mixed with the honey it becomes a source of energy. The mixture's exact ratio depends on your taste and the size of the cup. First add the honey to the water until it tastes sweet enough, and then add the vinegar until it tastes like hot apple cider (more or less). Take it a few times a day—the more the better.

- Avoid tea, coffee, cream, and alcohol before singing, as these can have a dehydrating effect on you.

- And above all, REST!

THE SINGER'S UTILITY KIT

The utility kit for a singer isn't nearly as extensive as for other types of touring musicians, but it's just as vital.

- A light source (like a flashlight or a clip-on book light from Radio Shack)
- A small notepad
- A box of pens
- A box of pencils with erasers
- A box of magic markers
- A couple of bottles of Entertainer's Secret
- A mild fruit drink (nonacidic)
- Honey
- A lemon or lemon substitute
- Tea
- Throat lozenges
- Aspirin or Advil
- A towel

CHAPTER 15

The Touring Keyboard Player

Regardless of whether it's playing in a local club band or touring with a superstar artist, the keyboard player has the most unique and usually the mostly unheralded position in the band. They have the most complicated gear, require the most setup time, and need to have more technical expertise than anyone else on the stage simply to operate their instruments—and they are usually the most musically educated player in the band. It's no wonder that most MDs are keyboard players.

Many times, the keyboard position is the most technically challenging, requiring a setup that far exceeds that of anyone else onstage in terms of amount of gear and its sophistication. That's why a keyboard tech may in some cases be elevated to a position that's more like a technical director, since the keyboard rig may interface with audio and video playback and even the stage lighting via MIDI.

Then again, maybe all the artist requires for the tour is a single keyboard with a traditional piano and organ patch. Either way, keyboard teching requires a unique expertise that not many backline techs can fulfill. Let's look two possible keyboard-tech scenarios.

Keyboard techs are expensive, and in this new touring economy, it's all too possible that you'll have to tech yourself on some tours. Here are some tips to make sure that your gear works perfectly show after show.

Keep a spare battery for all devices that use one for internal memory backup (see **Fig. 15.1**). This includes keyboards, samplers, computers, and just about any device that holds presets. Many times, these batteries aren't easily found on the road, so make sure you purchase spares before the tour begins. Be aware that your equipment can exhibit some unusual symptoms that can easily be misdiagnosed as some other type of problem altogether when these batteries begin to fail.

Fig. 15.1: A memory backup battery in a computer.

Have a backup keyboard ready just in case. Keyboards are incredibly robust and reliable these days, but sometimes the unexpected does happen. Even if you don't have room to set up your backup, at least have the case with the backup nearby.

Have a backup of your sounds. Most modern keyboards allow you to back up your sounds with a Compact Flash (CF) or SmartMedia flash memory card (see **Fig. 15.2**). Have a backup of all your sounds ready for the day your keyboard or sound module loses its mind and wipes your sounds from its memory. Having all your sounds on flash media also makes it easy to load everything into a new or a rental keyboard.

Fig. 15.2: A smart-card memory stick.

Program a set of backup sounds on another keyboard. Just in case the instrument with your main sounds should fail, having a set of the most critical sounds on your backup keyboard or sound module(s) is a wise alternative. They may not be exactly the same sounds, but at least they'll get you through the show.

Have a set of phone numbers handy of repair techs or factory service departments. If one of your instruments fails, you'll probably need expert help to get it back in service, and sometimes a mere phone call can get you out of a rough spot.

Use DeoxIT D5 on electronic connections like jacks. DeoxIT (see **Fig. 11.1** in chapter 11) is a space-age contact cleaner that keeps your electronic connects corrosion free. Simple corrosion, or metal oxidation (commonly known as rust) is the number one problem when it comes to metal-on-metal connections like jacks and plugs and old analog relays (like the kind used in Leslie-speaker motors). Any time a jack crackles, give it a quick shot of DeoxIT, work the plug in and out a few times, and if nothing is mechanically wrong with the jack or plug itself, the crackle will disappear like magic. This is especially important to do even on jacks you don't use that often, like amplifier insert jacks, which can cause an amp to drop in level or change tone at the slightest hint of corrosion. DeoxIT can still be found at any electronic-parts store like Radio Shack and sometimes even in some large drugstores.

Carry plenty of spares. You have to be prepared for the most common malfunctions, and you should never assume that you'll be lucky enough to be able to get replacements quickly on the road. Being prepared is the best way to keep a simple breakdown from stopping a show.

Place a piece of tape over any unused input or output jacks on the rear of your keyboards. You want to do this so that if you're in a hurry to set up, you won't accidentally connect something to the wrong jack. This is such an easy but overlooked trick, and it can really save you a lot of time by avoiding those moments when nothing works and you finally figure out that it's because of a misconnected plug. You think that this scenario will never happen to you, but sooner or later it will.

Put together a wiring harness for quick and easy setup (described next).

THE QUICK SETUP

If you have an extensive keyboard rig that requires a lot of setup, there are some tricks you can use to speed up the process as well as make everything more reliable. Consider trying these items.

1 If you're playing clubs that don't have much room onstage, the more setup you can do off-stage, the easier it will be for everyone on it. Nothing's harder than trying to set up with a bunch of empty cases lying around.

2 Place all your power strips and extension cords onstage first where you'll be setting up, before you even set your boards onstage.

3 If you're using keyboard amplification instead of relying on monitors, place your amplification on the stage next. This includes any mixer, power amp, speaker cabinet, or amplifier you need. Connect as much of the gear together as you can (like speaker cabinets to head, or mixer to power amp).

4 Run any cables from the mixer/amp to where the keyboards will be. To make your cable runs easier, consider either buying prefab snakes, making one by bundling the cables you normally use together with plastic cable ties, or using a plastic cable conduit like those made by Audioskin or Hosa (see **Fig. 15.3**). Avoid running audio cables and power cables together in the same bundle, since that could cause noise or hum in the audio. Make sure that you label everything so you know which cable goes to which keyboard.

Fig. 15.3: A wire loom.

5 Place your keyboards on their stands. To make this go faster, make sure you mark exactly where the height adjustment is for your playing style on your stand, so you'll always come back to the same place.

6 Connect the cables to the keyboards. Avoid winding your cables around the stand like a barber's pole, since doing so will take a lot of extra time to break down and you'll hate yourself if you have to replace a cable during the show. Some Velcro straps like the ones used for mic cables can attach your cables neatly.

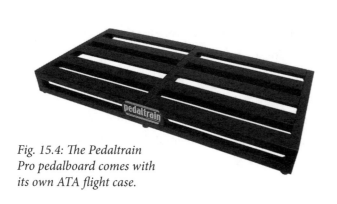

Fig. 15.4: The Pedaltrain Pro pedalboard comes with its own ATA flight case.

7 Make your life easier by taking a cue from guitarists the world over, and mount your pedals on a pedalboard. Have a few pedals? You may have multiple volume and sustain pedals that are always moving around. Having a pedalboard will make your setup and teardown easier, and your pedals will always be in the same place, and stay there. You can make one yourself, or just buy one from any number of vendors (see **Fig. 15.4**).

Fig. 15.5: A rackmountable
uninterruptible power supply.

8 Use an uninterruptible power supply (UPS) to provide clean power to your keyboard gear (see **Fig. 15.5**). Clean power is important because almost every piece of gear that a keyboard player uses contains a computer processor. A UPS can keep that power clean and your problems to a minimum. This is especially important if the stage lighting happens to be running off the same power leg as your keyboards. Remember that keyboards and computers take too much time to boot, reload, and reconfigure during a show, and since it's imperative to keep everything operating continuously during a show, the UPS will do that for you in the event of a momentary power failure.

THE KEYBOARD PLAYER'S UTILITY KIT

As Murphy's Law states, "If something can go wrong, it will go wrong!" so you have to be prepared for any eventuality during a show. Things break, but a pro is always ready. Having the items on the following list will prepare you for just about anything. Each item should be considered just as essential to playing a session as your keyboard is. Don't forget the hand truck or furniture mover to save your and your roadies' backs.

- An extra volume pedal
- An extra sustain pedal
- A spare keyboard stand
- A hand truck or furniture mover
- A light source (like a flashlight or a clip-on book light from Radio Shack)
- Gaffer's or duct tape
- Superglue
- Several extra MIDI cables
- An extra USB cable
- At least 2 extra 10' instrument cables (1/4" to 1/4")
- An extra 5' cable
- RCA-to-RCA cable
- Various cable adapters, like 1/4" to RCA, RCA to 1/4", and 1/4" to XLR

- 2 direct boxes, each with a ground-lift switch (always best to bring your own if you have some that you like)
- An extra power cable
- An extra power strip
- An AC extension cord (or two)
- Extra memory cards for your keyboards and sound modules
- Spare 9V batteries
- Spare AA batteries
- A spare universal 9V wall wart
- A small notepad
- A few pens
- A few pencils with erasers
- A few magic markers
- A towel

Your Keyboard Tech

The more sophisticated your rig, the more likely you are to have a keyboard tech. Artists and MDs are sensitive to the fact that keyboards are a different animal from anything else onstage and require an additional helping hand as a result. Let's take a look at what you can expect from a keyboard tech.

WHERE TO FIND A TECH

As I've said in the previous chapters, techs are normally found through word of mouth or are sometimes hired through repair shops, but when it comes to keyboards, techs with recording and MIDI chops may be hired through a recording studio as well.

Care should be taken when hiring a tech that lacks road experience, however, since the practical knowledge gained on the road is so different from that gotten in the studio. If a piece of gear doesn't work in the studio, a tech has the ability to take the time to troubleshoot while everyone around for him waits for him to get things back up and running. This is an unacceptable situation on the road, though, and some otherwise very good techs are unable to take the pressure of "the show must go on" mantra.

In the event that you can't find the tech you need through word of mouth, there are alternatives. You can take a look on Crewspace.com (a private, invitation-only job site for qualified [meaning experienced] touring professionals), roadie.net, and roadjobs.com.

WHAT TO LOOK FOR IN A TECH

A keyboard tech toes that fine line between being the pure tech that's an electronics and software boffin, and a player that knows how to use everything. That's why it's important to find someone who is just as musical as he is technical.

Usually a player looks for someone who can handle his particular technical side, but you want to find someone that will do it in a musical way. A player doesn't want to have to ask you to do something another way because what you did doesn't work smoothly during the performance. If you can find someone who's musical enough to understand that, and make it so you can just walk in and easily understand how what he did works in performance, that's what you want. They have to know what parts you're playing, what key you're playing them in, and when you're using different instruments and how you're using them. —Terry Lawless

More so than with any other member of your crew, you have to be comfortable with the personality of the tech. It's not impossible to work with someone you don't like, but it is uncomfortable. Who wants that situation when you have to spend so much time together over the course of a tour?

I want a tech that is going to be as conscientious at the gig as I am. I expect whomever I'm working with to be really quick, and to be listening to me all the time (especially during rehearsal), because if there's one thing that I hate, it's having to repeat myself. I expect them to get it the first time. I like someone who's knowledgeable at programming. I like to program all my own synths and stuff, but if I'm on the other side of the stage programming one of the other synths or if I'm in the front of house and I say, "Hey can you bring the filter cutoff down?" I want them to know how to do that. Most of the guys I've worked with have been able to do it or at least figure it out pretty quickly. If they can't figure it out, then they're not there very long.

As far as an audio tech, because I do a lot of digital audio stuff, too, I like them to be able to be musical. If I say, "I need you to do this at the beginning of bar 6, beat 3," they know what I'm talking about. It's rare to find someone that musical, because if they are, they're usually playing with someone. But if you can get someone that knowledgeable, it's a great thing.
—Paul Mirkovich

And finally, you don't want a tech who has the attitude that he can do your job better than you can. Most techs are former players and many are great in their own right, but being a tech means they must suppress those feelings for the job at hand. If you get the slightest hint that your potential tech is a frustrated player, it's time to move on.

Which brings me to another point that's a well-understood rule of the road. As a tech, you want to let the player know that you know a lot about what you're doing, but without coming off like a player. They'll feel comfortable if they know you can play some, but you never say that. That's a cardinal sin. I know a lot of techs that don't work just because they come off too much as a player and not enough as a tech. —Terry Lawless (who knows, because he's a great keyboard player as well as tech)

So be careful who you hire. Make sure that you get references, and follow them up. And be sure that you feel comfortable with your tech before having him sign on. After all, he's your security blanket during the tour.

THE TECH'S RESPONSIBILITIES

Many times, keyboard techs are required to do so much more than just set up and maintain the keyboards, depending on the sophistication of the keyboard setup. As soon as you get MIDI, computers, and audio playback involved, it's an entirely new ball game. Here's what you can expect from a tech.

- He'll have all your gear set up, checked out, and ready to go by soundcheck.
- He'll make sure that all computers and synchronization gear is in working order, and that all cables and wireless systems work flawlessly.
- Before each show, he'll replace the batteries in the wireless transmitter for portable keyboards and in any pedals that use batteries.
- During the show the tech is alert to the playing status of the keyboard player, and is always ready to spring into action if a piece of gear malfunctions.
- Techs may be involved in the keyboard player's performance during a show, actively controlling effects or patches at various points in the songs so that the player doesn't have to think about doing it.
- The tech may help with getting sounds together for the tour. Many techs get song files a couple of weeks before rehearsals begin so that they can copy sounds and loops. This may include trying to replicate sounds originally made by older gear on newer keyboards, or adapting samples originally done on an older unit to work on a newer one.

- The tech may serve as the DAW operator, working with recording applications like Logic or Pro Tools to cue any audio backing tracks or loops for the band to play against.
- He may program any MIDI configurations that might be required, and make sure that program changes take place on cue during the show.
- He may operate the gear that receives timecode from the FOH position that synchronizes any audio, video, or lighting cues.
- If he doesn't tune a real piano himself (in the event that you use one on the tour), he'll supervise the rental and/or tuning.
- He'll make you feel secure and at ease with his technical expertise. Some wtechs believe that 80 percent of their job is psychological, since the player who doesn't have to worry about the intricacies of the gear can just concentrate on performing.
- He'll tear down the rig immediately after the show. Most band gear is loaded onto the truck first, so everything has to be packed and on it within about 45 minutes after the last notes of the last song.

THE TECH'S TOOLBOX

Besides the spares listed in "The Keyboard Player's Utility Kit" sidebar above, many keyboard techs include the following additional items in their toolbox:

- Spare computers
- Spare rackmounted effects
- Spare keys for various keyboards
- A soldering iron
- Solder
- A variety of screws, washers, and nuts
- Additional onboard and flash memory cards for computers, keyboards, and sound modules
- An audio cable tester
- A computer and network cable tester
- Extra internal and external hard drives
- A crimping tool and RJ-45 connectors for making network cables
- Heat sinks
- Nut drivers
- Tweezers

- Chip extractors
- Chip inserter
- A desoldering tool
- A grounding strap
- Dust-off (compressed air in a can)
- An adjustable mirror
- Electrical tape
- A solder stand
- A third hand (a device that holds a piece to be soldered)
- Extra network cables
- Extra Firewire and USB cables
- Extra monitor cables
- Various audio, network, and computer adaptors
- Boot CDs for all gear in the rig
- Software diagnostic tools
- A set of torque screwdrivers (needed to open Apple cases)

COMMUNICATING WITH YOUR TECH

Most players and techs work out a series of head or hand signals with each other so they can communicate during the show. While the player can usually get the tech's attention by using head or hand signals, it's sometimes difficult for the tech to get the attention of the player. One way to accomplish this is by using a small indicator light with a red filter over it (so it doesn't interfere with the stage lighting), which is put in a place that the player can easily see. In any event, all signals should all be worked out beforehand so that neither the player nor the tech gets frustrated during the show.

Keep Your Gear Reliable

Touring is completely different from playing on the weekends in your local clubs or recording in your own or someone else's studio. Reliability is the key, which is something that becomes increasingly difficult as the sophistication of the keyboard rig increases. That's why it's so important to keep your rig as simple as the gig will allow. Having fewer components means that there are fewer things to go wrong, troubleshooting will be

Fig. 15.6: A computer with backup.

Fig. 15.7: A Hammond organ with a Leslie speaker and backup.

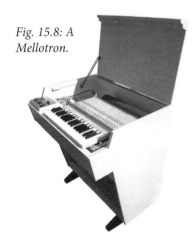

Fig. 15.8: A Mellotron.

Fig. 15.9: A Muse Receptor 2

easier when something does malfunction, and setup and teardown will be simplified.

Remember that specialty gear requires specialty techs. A rig that leans heavily on computers and revolves around a certain piece of software requires a computer-savvy tech with knowledge of that particular software app (see **Fig. 15.6**). A rig that uses a real Hammond organ and Leslie speaker (see **Fig. 15.7**) requires a tech who knows how to keep each running and how to fix and maintain each (a subspecialty in itself). And a rig that uses an exotic keyboard like a Mellotron (see **Fig. 15.8**) or Rhodes piano needs someone who has done more than hear them on recordings.

In an effort to eliminate computers that run virtual instruments or effects plug-ins from the stage, many players are now turning to the Muse Receptor instead (see **Fig. 15.9**). The unit enables sonic possibilities that are unavailable with a computer (such as layering of instruments and effects) and provides a condensed signal path that also eliminates onstage audio mixers. Check out museresearch.com for more information.

I used to use the laptop to play some VST synths before the Receptor came out. I think I might have been one of the first guys to do that. I used to run a few synths out of a software utility called V-Stack, and it was very buggy and would crash all the time. Then the laptop would overheat and decide not to work. It was a pain in the butt, so I moved to the Receptor as soon as it came out. I have run tracks from laptops live on occasion, but I really don't like to be the guy pushing the buttons to run digital audio on a tour. I'd rather think about playing. —Paul Mirkovich

CHAPTER 16

The Touring Horn Player

I n some ways, horn players (here, referring to both brass and reeds)
have it a bit easier than other touring musicians (except for singers)
in that they have less gear to worry about and a smaller range of
sonic choices to contend with. But as with everything on the road, what
isn't immediately obvious can be the part that trips you up. Learning
some of the tricks can be helpful as you head toward your first shows.
Traditionally, horn players are among the best sight-readers, most
exciting soloists, and finest on-the-spot arrangers, so you'll be expected to
bring a high level of musicianship with you to the stage. It's great to have a
reputation as a killer soloist, but it's even better to be able to work well as
part a section, in the spirit of the Memphis Horns or the Tower of Power
horns. Why? Horn players work, but horn sections work *a lot*.

Real music played by real players is never going to go away, and
there is almost nothing as exciting as a world-class horn section playing
onstage. Established horn sections are an artist's dream—you come in
already cookin', like a greased machine ready to add your flavor, bring the
intensity up a notch, and send the song into overdrive. And after all, that's
what a great show is all about.

Your Case

Protection of your instrument is always a number one priority, because the last thing you want is to have your precious instrument damaged from the rigors of the road. It's recommended that you budget at least 10 percent of the value of your instrument when purchasing a case. Keep in mind that the first time you have to repair your instrument because you cheaped out with an inexpensive case will cost more than buying an expensive case in the first place.

SOME PRECAUTIONS

Even with a great case, you still should take a few extra precautions just to be sure that your horn always stays safe. Since the bell flare is the most fragile part of your instrument, you should put something inside it for transit. A Styrofoam cone from an art store, a warm-up mute, or even an inflatable beach ball all provide the additional support required for safe transit.

Also, put as much padding around the instrument as possible. A safe instrument is one that has no movement inside the case and is tight with the lid closed.

FLYING WITH YOUR CASE

Smaller horns like trumpets, flutes, alto saxes, and even tenor saxes are some of the few instruments that can be safely carried on a flight these days, but it's not always a given. That being said, if you observe the following tips from the Horn Guys (hornguys.com), you may find yourself on the plane with your horn securely in the overhead. This is assuming that you're flying with a soft case for your instrument rather than an ATA flight case, which will almost always have to be checked as baggage.

- Choose a seat that boards relatively early so that you aren't the last one getting on a full plane with full overhead bins. This may mean printing out a boarding pass on your computer the night before your flight leaves, if possible.

- Carry nothing else on besides your instrument. If your horn is a bit over the regulation size, you don't want to make things more difficult by carrying on a bunch of other crap, too. You and your horn and a jacket are enough. Don't abuse the rules more than you have to—simply bend them a bit.

- Dress professionally and in a businesslike fashion. You don't want to look like some derelict slacker stoner dude who might cause a problem. You want to look like you know what you're doing, and that you have done this before. You're a professional, not a weasel.

- Use a case that has a shoulder strap, and put it over the shoulder that is opposite the ticket taker at the gate. They might not even notice until you get past, and by then they're greeting the next passenger. If you hold the ticket in your right hand to give to the agent on your right side, the case goes over your left shoulder and you casually turn to the right as you go by to hide the case from full view.

- Don't expect special treatment just because your instrument is large and expensive. There are a lot of people boarding the plane who paid more for their ticket than you did.

- If you have the air miles or the cash to upgrade to business class, do it.

- Carry a copy of the American Federation of Musicians' correspondence with the TSA that you can download at www.hornguys.com/TSALetter. pdf. Also, check out the article at the TSA website about carrying musical instruments on board (www.tsa.gov/travelers/airtravel/assistant/editorial_1235.shtm).

[The case I use] depends on the gig. If I'm just playing tenor, I will carry it on in like a Walt Johnson lightweight flight case. The reality of air travel now is that they can and will take your instrument away from you, and you have to be prepared for the fact that it might end up in the baggage compartment of the plane. —Ed Wynne

Here are some additional travel tips from the Horn Guys.

"If you run into trouble and face being refused boarding unless you check your priceless horn in its gig bag, be nice, and memorize this:

1 Tell a very concise sob story: "On the last flight, there was no problem," or "The last time I had to check it, it sustained $200 damage, and your company would not pay for it," or "I fly about six weeks a year, and this is the first time anyone has mentioned it" and so on. Be concise and calm. Make something up ahead of time, but keep it short. George Carlin memorized his routines—so should you.

2 Then tell them (concisely) what you want: "I'd like to carry this on and put it in the coat closet . . ." (or behind the last bulkhead row, or in the overhead bin) ". . . where it will surely fit fine. It always has. What kind of plane is this? 737? Oh yeah, it always fits fine. May I carry it on?"

3 Then, quickly, before you get an answer, say the following—word for word—with lots of eye contact, a big smile, and a flirtatious playful tone:

"If you can't do it, I'd certainly understand."

<short pause>

"But if you *could*, I'd *really* appreciate it."

<short pause>

"Don't get into any trouble, now."

Practice the preceding lines in front of a friend. Memorize them. Make them your mantras. This is your key to success. Trust me. I sweet-talked my way out of paying Lufthansa's 125-euro excess-baggage fee for a giant contrabass trombone case in Frankfurt using this technique. You see, instead of begging, you're *giving* the power to the gate agent, and they like that. They deal with people all day who bitch at them for every crazy reason imaginable. You want to create the most positive moment of personal interaction in their day. If you do, everyone wins and goes away feeling good. And you get what you want."

Fig. 16.1: An ATA-standard flight case for multiple trumpets.

While you might not have a problem with a trumpet or an alto as a carry-on, it's still a good idea to have an ATA-standard flight case for your instrument (see **Fig. 16.1**), especially if you'll be doing a lot of flying, or if you're traveling with multiple instruments.

If you need more information about the different types of flight cases available, see chapter 7 for more details.

Additional Carry-ons

It's a good idea to place your mouthpieces, reeds, and neck straps in a separate carry-on in the event that your checked horn gets damaged or doesn't show up at the other end of the line. This way you have at least some of your key playing components if you have to borrow an instrument.

What I learned from that was not to check my mouthpieces, reeds, neck straps, and all that stuff. I now pack them in a little bag in my carry-on. Because they're metal and they're pointy, I get stopped everywhere—so I leave a reed on so I can blow through it for Security so they understand what it is. —Ed Wynne

Being Miked

One of the biggest pains for a horn player is being miked onstage. Although standard vocal mics like Shure SM58s work well for brass and reed instruments, most players hate blowing into anything connected to a fixed stand, since it limits playing comfort. As a result, sometimes it's in your best interest to take matters into your own hands.

Fig. 16.2: An SD Systems LCM89 clip-on mic.

Many horn players are now carrying their own clip-on mics, which are available from a number of manufacturers. They have the dual function of sounding great while increasing your playing comfort (see **Fig. 16.2**). Most of them are condenser mics, which means they need to be powered (have "phantom power") to work, which all house or monitor mixing consoles can supply. You might want to purchase an external AC or battery power supply just to be sure that you're covered for other situations when you aren't on tour, or if you'll be touring in some third-world country where you're never sure what the sound system will be like.

I bring an Electro-Voice clip-on microphone specially designed for wireless transmitters. For solos, we want to use a wireless as much as possible, so we can bring the soloist to the front of the stage to interact with the crowd and that kind of stuff. This mic is compatible with the wireless packs that are supplied by the sound company. Some of the mics that come with the wireless packs don't sound that good in my opinion, so this gives me something that I know will sound good and be consistent from gig to gig. —Ed Wynne

While most mics are condensers, SDS Systems (www.sdsystems.com) is one of the few companies that offer a dynamic (nonpowered) mic that is especially designed for brass and reed instruments. The company also offers a wide range of condenser clip-on mics, all designed specifically for a particular musical instrument.

Hearing Yourself Onstage

On large superstar tours, horn players may be given their own in-ear monitors with their own separate mix, which most players love once they get used to it. Most of the time, though, the horn players (if you're in a section) will have a single mix between them and are left to work out their own balance. This is something that most players like to do anyway. Great sections mix themselves and don't depend on the monitor or FOH mixer to do it for them.

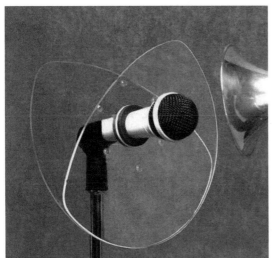

Fig. 16.3: A Soundback reflector.

That being said, many horn players have difficulty hearing themselves even with roaring floor monitors, because there's nothing on the stage to reflect the sound back to the player's ears, unlike the way they're used to hearing things. Luckily, there's an inexpensive solution called a sound reflector. A sound reflector is a piece of clear Plexiglass that mounts either directly on the bell of the horn or on a mic stand (see **Fig. 16.3**). The idea is to reflect sound back at the player so that he doesn't have to rely on monitors. You can either make your own or buy one of the many commercial versions available (the Ploeger Sound Mirror, the Soundback reflector, or the Note Bandit).

The Touring String Player

hile on the surface bringing a string section on the road may seem like an extravagance that few artists or bands can afford, more and more artists are doing it. String sections like the Siren Electric String Quartet (which has toured with Gnarls Barkley, P. Diddy, and Simply Red) and the Rock 'n' Roll Strings (Dave Matthews, Brian Wilson, and Wilco) can and do work constantly. Even though it's still a common practice to pick up additional players at each tour stop, the core elements that are on the tour are essential to a tight-sounding section.

The Difference with Pop Music

While most string players are familiar with the regimen and standards of the classical world, the pop/rock world requires a different mind-set. Certainly, the classical training is essential to the tone and intonation required, but there's more to playing pop/rock than that.

A NEW CHALLENGE

Many classically trained string players can be snobby and narrow minded about the value of pop music or the talent of its stars. Now is the time to open your mind to a different kind of challenge. They are two different types of music, and you do a disservice to both if you diss either one. Just enjoy the opportunity to play something different and explore a new test of your technique.

Usually, the artist wants you to make your performance look effortless, because your look and attitude onstage are also important. What you might be able to get away with in a large orchestra setting will immediately show up in a pop show, with frequent camera close-ups projected on the big screen. If you look grumpy or slovenly during a pop show, more people will notice, while looking churlish or testy during a classical concert might be interpreted as being serious or focused.

But that's not all. In certain situations, the ability to improvise may be important. That's not something taught at a conservatory, so it's usually a skill that's attained postgraduation. And there are a lot more visual cues in pop than you might be used to, so you always have to be paying attention.

There's a very small percentage of string players that can bridge the classical and the improvisational world, and there's an even smaller percentage that can do both of those things well. —Heather Lockie

And finally, remember that you're there to support the artist or band, and the audience is there to see them, not you. You're part of the icing on the cake, not the cake itself.

Your Instrument on the Road

Touring can be hard on an instrument, so here are some tips to keep it in tip-top shape for every show. You're most likely aware of these, but touring intensifies the potential for a small problem that's been overlooked to turn into a catastrophe.

• Put a dampened instrument humidifier in your case to keep the moisture content of the wood the same. This will lessen the chance of thermal shock affecting your instrument as it moves through changing environments and atmospheric conditions. Be sure that any wet material does not directly contact the violin or the case itself.

- Wipe off your violin with a cotton cloth every time you put it away so that the rosin dust does not build up and become difficult to remove later.
- Loosen your bow when you're finished playing at the end of the show, and tighten it before your warm-ups for the next show.
- Before you play, wash your hands to get rid of the oily buildup on your fingers. This keeps your instrument free of fingerprints that can easily be seen on the video displays during those high-definition close-ups.
- When changing strings, rub some graphite or the lead of a pencil into the guides on your top nut and string indentations on the bridge. This helps the strings tighten more easily.
- Don't store your instrument near a heater or air conditioner. Even an outside wall can cause the temperature to rise or fall to an unsafe level.
- Avoid any temperature or humidity extremes.

THE STRING PLAYER'S UTILITY KIT

Just about every string player brings most of these items already, but it's always good to have a list.

- A digital tuner
- Lots of rosin
- An extra bow
- A violin humidifier
- A few extra sets of strings
- A cotton or soft microfiber towel
- A small notepad
- A few pens
- A few pencils
- A few magic markers

Making Your Instrument Louder

One of the most difficult things for a sound engineer to do is to mix a bunch of relatively quiet acoustic instruments (strings) against an amplified band, and get them to a level that the audience can hear them. It's no picnic for the string players, either, as they struggle to hear

Fig. 17.1: An L.R. Baggs bridge pickup.

themselves against the din. In fact, one of the reasons that the strings are usually placed behind the band onstage or behind a Plexiglass wall (or both) is to keep some audio separation between the two.

Most engineers would much prefer that all strings have a pickup in order to keep the isolation at its maximum. Pickups can be separated into two categories:

• **Permanent pickups** are built into either the original or a replacement bridge. These can sound great but must be fitted by a luthier. While this might seem to be an extreme solution, there are more brands of permanent pickups than you might think, with models made by L. R. Baggs (see **Fig. 17.1**), Shatten, and Fishman to name a few.

I used to have an L. R. Baggs pickup, which was pretty good, but now I have this pretty amazing pickup called a Shertler. The frequency response is really even, but you have to have it installed in your bridge. It's a great-sounding pickup. — Heather Lockie

• **Temporary pickups** can be attached to and taken off of your instrument relatively quickly and as needed. As a general statement, the audio quality isn't as good as the permanent bridge type, but they do allow you to use your favorite instrument rather than a secondary instrument that's been relegated to "electric-only" status. The Kremona violin pickup (see **Fig. 17.2**) is a highly regarded yet inexpensive (less than $100) example of a temporary pickup using a piezoelectric pickup element.

Fig. 17.2: A Kremona piezoelectric pickup.

Another is the Audio-Technica ATM350, which is actually a microphone that's been specially adapted for string applications (see **Fig. 17.3**) that clips onto the bridge.

Sometimes the sound engineer would prefer to use a lavaliere mic like the kind that newscasters wear to amplify your instrument. Be aware that the clips of these mics sometimes have teeth on them so they'll better grip the newscaster's clothes, but those teeth have to be padded so your instrument doesn't get scratched. Just cut a piece of chamois to the proper dimensions and that should do the job nicely.

There's also sort of a hybrid type of semipermanent mic like those by Realist Acoustics (see **Fig. 17.4**) that mounts

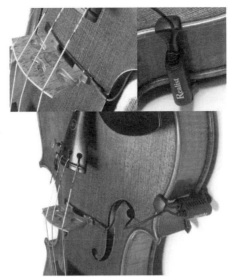

Fig. 17.3: The Audio-Technica ATM350.

Fig. 17.4: A Realist violin mic.

underneath the bridge. Many players love the sound of this type of pickup, but it does mean that it can be removed only if the strings are loosened first.

Hearing Yourself Onstage

Like all other players onstage, string players may be given two choices for monitoring: traditional monitor wedges or in-ear monitors. Most string players much prefer in-ears if given a choice, since in-ears have the added benefit of blocking the sound of any of the louder instruments onstage, which makes tuning easier. In-ears enable you to keep the volume level reasonable, as compared with monitor wedges, which usually have to blast to keep up with the volume onstage.

In terms of the mix, it's a given that a string player wants to hear the other string players in order to blend well, but all string players like to hear an instrument with a solid tuning, like a piano or keyboard, to tune against. In the absence of a keyboard, a rhythm guitar and bass in the monitors is usually sufficient.

We really have to hear the things that are the least tunable in themselves, like a piano or a keyboard, because they have a set tuning. We can modify our tuning to match it if we can hear it. —*Heather Lockie*

PART 3

THE INTERVIEWS

Grecco Buratto

Grecco Buratto is the thinking man's guitar player; he's spiritual by nature, which makes his integration into road life all the more interesting. Besides playing sessions with Earth, Wind & Fire, Pink, and Boyz II Men, Grecco has composed for movies and television commercials, but like most musicians, playing in front of an audience is in his blood. After touring with Anastacia, k.d. lang, Enrique Iglesias, Airto and Flora, Sergio Mendez, and Keiko Matsui, Grecco describes his unique road routine.

What was the first road gig that you did?

That would be Sergio Mendez from 2001 to 2003. I got the gig because I was playing in the Brazilian scene around Los Angeles where I played a few gigs with the Sergio's MD. He asked me to audition, which turned out to be an actual show in Miami. He'd been trying to get me an audition for over a year but it never worked out for one reason or another.

What kind of gear did you use with Sergio?

I was doing a lot of demos and low-budget records at the time. I had a Bradshaw system (Custom Audio Electronics pedal switching system), which is what I took to that first gig because I wanted to sound just like the record since it was my audition. After a while, though, I realized that wasn't such a good thing to use because of some of the weight limits that we were under, so I had Bob [Bradshaw, the president of Custom Audio Electronics] build me a pedalboard that was the most basic I could think of, yet it had everything I needed. That's actually what I still use today on the road. It's just a volume pedal, a distortion pedal, reverb, chorus, wah, and an A/B box so I can go between electric and acoustic guitar. That's it.

You must've been doing mostly fly dates then.
For Sergio, yes. I've done bus tours with Enrique Iglesias and k.d. lang, but even then I found that I didn't want to bring my Bradshaw rig on the road. It didn't really make a difference in my playing or my sound for those gigs.

With Enrique I just took my basic pedalboard, added a delay pedal to it, and two amps [a Matchless DC-30 and VHT Pitbull head with two cabinets]. I did take my Bradshaw rig when I did Anastacia, because I felt I really needed the versatility of the rack on that gig. Even though they were fly dates, they flew all of our gear to Europe, and it helped that I really trusted my guitar tech on that tour.

What guitars do you usually take out with you?
It depends. With Anastacia I took a Strat, a Les Paul, and a Yamaha-type Strat that I used on a couple of songs. While I was with Enrique, I connected with a company called First Act, and I used those guitars on the tour. I love the way they look and the way they sound, and the company has treated me really well.

What do you look for in a guitar tech?
I'm a bit of a control freak in the sense that I have a particular way that I like everything to be set up, like the way the cables are wrapped and things like that. I know that most of the time a load-out is a big rush for a tech, so I had to learn to let go of a lot of that. So now I'm not really picky, because I realize that the setup won't be exactly the way that I'd do it most of the time.

What do you take with you on fly dates?
Again it depends on the gig. I was playing with Airto and Flora, and at first I used to take my nylon string guitar, an electric guitar, and my pedalboard. Then I realized that unless you're on in-ears, nylon- or steel-string acoustic guitar is an exercise in detachment because rarely do I get to hear myself that well. So I stopped taking the nylon string and just took a guitar that would cut through everything, and that was the Les Paul.

That way there was one less thing to carry around, I could carry it on the plane in a gig bag, and I made it work just fine for the gig.

Are you usually on in-ears?

For the bigger pop tours like Anastacia and Enrique, they use in-ears. With k.d. it's all wedges, but the volume is surprisingly quiet.

What's it like going back and forth between k.d. and Enrique?

I like doing it because it's different, but they're as far away from each other as you can imagine. k.d. has an older crowd, and Enrique has teenagers to thirty-somethings, and the majority of them are women. Actually, that's true for k.d., too. *[Laughs.]*

What's it like playing to an audience filled with females?

I don't know if I have any feeling on that. I'm a support musician and I'm backing the artist. All the eyes are on the artist, although we do get our little shine time. If you're in the phase of your life where you want to party, it's great. After a while, I got tired of it.

I tend to look for meaning in everything I do, and I don't want to fall into escapism the way a lot of musicians do. Sometimes you're playing music that doesn't exactly resonate with you, but you have to pay your bills so you end up going into alcohol, drugs, sex or all of the above so that you don't have to think about the things that you're not happy about. I did it myself for a little while, but it got to a point where I needed something else that was more fulfilling.

I remember doing some video promo and feeling that the energy was pretty bad and I felt bad in the environment. A week later I met k.d. at a session for her album, and it was one of the best experiences in my professional life because she treats everyone with such respect. You're brought in because she wants you to add what you bring to her music. That's when I realized that in the pop world, it's to your employer's advantage to make you feel disposable, and I needed a gig that wasn't like that.

There are a lot of people that would kill for a gig like that.

I realize that it's L.A. and that if you don't want to do the gig, there are 50 other guys that can do it just as well. Well, there are and there aren't, because there's a lot more to the gig than just being able to play the music. At the end of the day, playing is not the main issue, because if you've been recommended for the gig, you can play. Everybody can play. The issue is, can you live with a person on the bus for the next six months? Are you a good hang? Are you a fun guy to be around, or are you a complainer? That's more important, in my opinion, than playing. But in pop music, you have to look a certain way. Everybody has to look great, but then you dress them all in black and put them at the back of the stage in the dark, and you get the feeling of, "What did we just go through all of that for?"

Have you done many auditions?

I've done like two cattle-call auditions in my life and I didn't get either one, partially because I don't like doing them, but mostly because I prefer that people call me for what they know I can do. Most of the times at an audition, they don't know what they want, and so there's more of a feeling like, "Impress me," in the room. I feel that if I'm recommended by someone, that should be enough.

I understand that in the world today you have to have a certain look. I get it, but I don't want to be part of that and I've been lucky enough that I haven't had to be part of that. I get called because of word of mouth now. Of course, sometimes a cattle call is to get some young kids that are eager to go out on the road for $500 a week.

Do you have anything that you do on the road to keep yourself entertained or sane?

I have a routine of things that I do every day. For a while I was on the move quite a bit. I'd go out for five weeks with Airto, then I'd come back for four days, then I'd go to the Ukraine with Keiko for a week, and so on. During that, I developed a checklist of things that I needed to do every day. It was a commitment to myself that went something like, "I'm going to learn Italian and French, go to the gym every day, do vocal exercises and practice the guitar." I had to do three of these things every day no matter where I was. When we'd get to a venue, I'd find a room that wasn't being used and just do what I needed to do. That's how I stay sane.

That's one of the reasons I like being on the road. You have a lot of time; actually, I have more time to myself on the road than when I'm in town. If we're going to the venue at 4 p.m. for soundcheck, even if you get up at 11 p.m., you still have five hours to fill, so I decided to use the time to get some of those self-improvement things accomplished.

When I went out with k.d., I got into yoga and meditation and I practiced those a lot. I think musicians are pretty disciplined to begin with, otherwise we'd never get good on our instruments in the first place. We have the dedication and the drive—it just has to be channeled beyond music.

What do you pack for the road?

I take a yoga mat, books, yoga manuals, and a couple of guitar music books. I'll actually take clothes out of my bag so I can take more books. If it's a longer tour, I'll take my Mbox, and I can't go without my laptop as well.

What was the best gig you ever did?

There were a few. There was one gig with Enrique at Wembley where I had just finished subbing as the MD for the first three weeks. It was the first time that the MD was not there in like eight years, so things were a little tense before this gig and I had to step into some big shoes. We started in South Africa, went to Europe, and Wembley was like week three or four, and that's where it all came together. The band played great, the setlist was tight, Enrique was great, and his family was there so it was a big deal for him.

Then I remember when I was first getting into yoga and meditation, I did a gig with k.d. where I was focusing on my breath the whole show. I remember looking at my hands playing, but I didn't feel as if it were me doing the playing. I was witnessing myself playing and it was amazing. I thought, "That's what I need to do every night." To me, the mark of a good show is when I don't remember most of it, because my brain was not there when it was happening.

Another with k.d. was at the Ryman Auditorium in Nashville. We had done a North American leg, an Australian leg, and a European leg, and this was the last leg for that year. She had a whole new band except for the drummer, and they were all my age [early 30s]. Her band before us had guys we all admired and who were our heroes, and that was the level that she'd been used to. Throughout that year it was a huge learning experience for us, but at the Ryman it felt like we owned our space and we were graduating. We played our butts off and we knew that we could do this. That felt amazing.

Walter Earl

A veteran of the road, Walter Earl has worked as a drum tech, stage manager, and tour manager for acts such as Siouxsie and the Banshees, and all their spin-off bands (drummer, Budgie), Jessica Simpson (drummer, Gorden Campbell), Marilyn Manson (drummer, Ginger Fish), and Fleetwood Mac (drummer, Mick Fleetwood). A longtime personal assistant and studio tech for legendary Black Sabbath drummer Bill Ward, Walter looks into the day-to-day duties of a modern drum tech and gives us an insight into the protocol of the road.

What are your responsibilities?

First, understand that there's the world of teching when you're doing clubs and small theaters, then there's the world of teching when you're on a huge production like OzzFest, and they are two completely different animals. When you travel overseas, it's another story as well, especially if you're using rental gear.

On a headlining tour, your day starts at between 10 a.m. and noon, when you get to the venue. The local loaders will bring the gear out on stage, where you'll unpack your boxes and determine exactly what needs to be done. You usually travel with a carpet that you marked the location on where all of your drums and cymbal stands sit during production rehearsals, so that's the first thing on your drum riser every day.

Sometimes the local crew wants to help, so if everything is marked, you can more or less call it out to them.

The rest of the day you may spend repairing something from the previous night, changing out the drumheads or cymbals, making sure that all your stuff is in good working condition and that it's clean (although you might work for a drummer that doesn't care much about how clean things are), and then tuning everything up. In between, you might have to get on the phone with your endorsers to order drumheads, cymbals, hardware, drums or drum sticks, and advance anything that might be coming up in the tour.

Once your guy gets on site, you take him through any problems that might have erupted the night before. Then you just get ready for your drummer to come up on stage for soundcheck or the show.

When the show starts you'll always sit either to the right or left of your drummer (as long as there's room on the stage), while the other techs are usually in the wings. You have to keep your eye on your guy all night, so that if there's any problems you can jump right in to get the problem resolved, although you really want to see things before they become problems.

You also want to be able to interface with the monitor engineer because you're the link between him and the drummer. That means you have to understand what your drummer wants to hear out of the monitors or in-ears. It's really important that you interface well with the monitor guy, because he's the guy under the most amount of stress on stage, so if you make his life easy, he'll go out of his way to make it easy for you and your guy.

Do you have to worry about any electronics?

For about 15 years you had to have a good knowledge of electronics and how triggering worked, but that was more through the late '80s and '90s. That being said, yesterday I did the Jimmy Kimmel show with Massive Attack and they had an acoustic drummer and an electronic drummer, and the drum tech shared both duties.

Nowadays drum techs may be asked to fire some samples or loops off, or asked to play percussion behind the drums. You sometimes wind up being the fifth member of the band without it ever being on record that that's the case.

What's different if you're an opening act?

If you're in an opening slot, it's a bit harder because you're going to be the last one to soundcheck right before doors. Nine times out of ten, the drummer or drum tech in the opening act tends to get the brunt of all the abuse because you have the most gear to move, but they only want to give up a certain amount of space in front of the headliner's drum riser. That's where it all comes down to diplomacy. You want to keep the headlining act's crew happy, because you have to commingle with them every day and share the same stage.

If you're going overseas, nowadays you'll rent gear [over there] instead of shipping over your American gear. On big tours you usually don't have to worry about rentals because there's a bigger budget, so they'll bring the gear over, but if that's not in the budget, then you're renting. That means they don't want a drum tech to come over with his big production box, so you'll have to bring like a fiber trap case or Home Depot toolbox with all the necessary tools like cymbal felts and tools and washers and nuts and bolts.

How often do you normally change heads?

Some guys want their heads changed every day, but a lot of the old-timers would rather play on the same heads until they break. A guy like Charlie Watts never changes heads and can go through a whole tour on the same set!

Do you tune the kit, or does the drummer?

Most guys will entrust you to tune their kit, although they might do some microtuning when they start soundcheck—although if my drummer trusts me with the tuning, he's really not needed around for soundcheck. He's still needed, but it just expedites the soundcheck.

What you want to do as a drum tech is to get your guy to a point where you're making all of those types of decisions for him. You kind of have to let that evolve, though. The best artist that you can work for is the one that can entrust you with their gear 100 percent.

What are the hardest gigs for you to do?

As far as the work goes, the smaller venues are the hardest, but as far as diplomacy and keeping your head, it's the big gigs because of the politics. On smaller tours you might be asked to do keyboards or play percussion or be the stage manager, so you're probably wearing multiple hats. If you're playing in Hollywood at some place like the Whiskey, the drum tech's job is twice as hard, because you load out the gear right onto the sidewalk amongst the crowd, so you have to keep an eye on all your gear as it's being packed up to make sure that nothing walks off.

On a theater tour, you may also be asked to break down the merchandising booth every night. There's usually only one merch guy on smaller tours and they're traveling with the crew, so nobody wants to wait around for him to break down since merchandising companies use an archaic way of counting every shirt (it's a little caveman-esque, but it works). The older, experienced guys usually help out wherever the help needs to be anyway, so that you can either get the show on the road or get the hell out of the venue faster at the end of the night.

With a new band on their first or second album, they're doing big clubs and small theaters, so your crew is anywhere from three to seven guys at the most. Three to seven guys can get along, but once you start to fill a deck with the amount of guys it takes to do a major production, you have to interface with a lot more people and you're expected to maintain an accepted protocol.

What's the protocol?

That means things like not cutting the line when waiting to eat at craft services or to take a shower, or waiting until the artist showers first, especially if they're not getting hotel rooms. So there are some courtesies that you usually learn through someone screaming at you at 2 o'clock in the morning, "Why'd you take the last towel? The artist didn't shower yet." When I did the last tour with Jessica Simpson, we supported Rascal Flatts and they provided us with production towels after the show every night, so we didn't have that problem.

As far as the bus goes, you never want to leave any of your stuff out in the aisle. It's dangerous at night with no lights on in the bus. When I started touring, they told you once to put your shoes in your bunk or a little storage area, and if you didn't listen, the next morning they were gone. You always want to clean up after yourself, and you don't want to go to sleep leaving your beer bottles or food out.

On small tours overseas, many newbies don't fare well if they're not tour savvy. The first thing is to try not to think like an American when you're in Europe. The first time you learn that is when you walk into a lift in Europe and it's a third the size of what you're used to, and the hotel hallways are smaller so you end up struggling with your big American luggage. When we first started touring Europe, all the food that was served cold over here was served warm there, and everything that was served warm here was served cold there. You'd do gigs and there'd be no ice because they didn't consider ice to be something important for a long time. The other thing is that you have to know how to read GMT time on your watch, which is essential for touring overseas. The new kids as well as some veterans just see the road as one big party.

What's in your workbox?

You can usually ask the company that your artist is endorsed by to supply you with all the parts you need, but if not, you go to Guitar Center to buy your spares. You want extra cymbal felt, an extra hi-hat clutch, extra tension rods, some wing nuts for the top of the cymbal stands, extra beaters, lots of extra heads, extra snare wires, maybe a spare snare hoop, and all the little nuts and bolts that are associated with a drum kit. You also need a good cordless reversible drill, and you might need a metronome and a set of headphones for your drummer.

I've also found that you can use the little copper chain that plumbers use and screw it down around the stands, or screw the drum legs directly into the deck. That way, nothing moves and you only need three to five minutes at the end of the show to unscrew everything so the local hands can take it out to a loading dock or parking lot. So I take a lot of that chain, too.

How many snare drums will you take?

You'll figure out in production rehearsals how many snare drums you need to travel with. You definitely keep an extra one on stage every night because it's easier to swap out a snare drum than it is to swap out a head. You usually have a backup for the spare snare, because that's something you might have to use for parts later in the tour. Sometimes you'll even have a spare kick drum, because the whole show can come to a screeching halt if you break a kick drumhead. You want to carry a couple of extra kick drum pads because if the head does break, you can use them to get through a song until there's a lull in the show to change it. Back in the day when ballads were a big thing, we'd usually swap a deeper snare as well.

The workbox is that big in shear size, because guitar workboxes wind up being a lot bigger than drum workboxes, but the more you have the better. You have to remember that anything that can go wrong on tour, will go wrong. The funny part is, when I first started, all you really needed was a drum key. [Laughs.]

What should a drummer look for in a tech?

You want someone who can identify issues before they become problems. You want to be able to hire someone who has the same kind of music vocabulary as you. You want to find someone that reads *Modern Drummer* or any of the drumming publications so that he stays ahead of the technology arc and can keep you ahead as a result. You want a drum tech that's mechanically inclined, knows the gear, and who can at least play a decent beat so the sound guys can get a balance from the kit during soundcheck.

How has touring changed from the time you started to the way it is now?
When I first started touring, we didn't have cell phones or computers, so you got on the phone and did everything from a landline. Believe it or not, all of those old tours before about 1995 were done without computers or Blackberrys or cell phones, and they still got done. You see new production guys come on the block and their heads are exploding because they're having a hard time, and you have to remind them that the whole touring industry was built prior to anyone having a Macbook Pro.

Travel has not gotten easier. Travel in a bus has gotten more luxurious and comfortable, but as far as airports go, it's a lot worse. The gear has gotten a lot better because the advances in technology are amazing, which goes to show that you can't reinvent the wheel, but you can reinvent all the things that hang off the wheel. The advances in sound and lights are remarkable, but for every one new thing, there seems to be a need for two new cases to put it in.

Communication between the artist and the drum companies has gotten better, too. The food still sucks, though. You still find the same caterers 20 years later making the same horrible food.

What do you pack in your suitcase when you go out on the road?
A lot of techs have adopted rugged clothing by North Face or Patagonia. Multipocket cargo pants are good, so you can keep a lot of stuff in your pockets at all times, especially when you travel internationally. A couple of Nike All Conditions Gear shoes are great, because you're going to be on your feet all day. And you can't forget an extra set of Rite Aid double insoles. You need a good hoodie and a good pair of work gloves, and some extralarge ziplock bags to put your dirty laundry into. Of course, you want to take your stage blacks [black clothing for the show].

One of the most important things is, you definitely want to take a pair of flip-flops, because the worst thing about the road is sharing showers. You might have 12 guys that hit a shower, which means that if you don't wear flip-flops, you'll wind up with a hellacious case of athlete's foot. A pair of Nike Aqua Socks work just as well. You've got to shower in those, because God knows what you're stepping on. Speaking of showers, when I first started touring in Europe, five plastic bags hung around a hose with a showerhead was considered a shower!

What about traveling internationally?

The first thing is, you never want to lose control of your passport when you travel, so you want to carry it close to you at all times. You don't want to put your passport in your bag, because that's too easily stolen or lost. Many tour managers will ask you for a scan of your passport, but a lot of guys are rightfully paranoid about that. If you do take a scan of your passport and it's on your computer, a lot of bad things can happen in the event that you lose it. If you do scan it, keep it on a server or a flash drive, but not on your hard drive. In general, you need the ability to keep all of your personal belongings with you at all times, because there are stories about guys having their stuff robbed out of a bus.

You also have to know to shut the roaming off on your cell phone when you're overseas so you don't come home to a $3,000 bill. The best thing is to go to the Orange, Vodaphone, or Virgin Mobile store and get a one-time "burner" phone. You just use it for that tour, and then pull the SIM out when the tour is over.

What was the worst tour you've ever been on?

I never really had a bad tour as a tech. As a player, it's a different story. *[Laughs.]* Festivals are a lot of work, because you have to interface with so many people, stay diplomatic, and stand your ground but understand that a lot of other people have to stand on that ground with you. Festivals in Europe are probably some of the hardest days that you can have.

Why in Europe?

They have a lot more festivals than we have here, but unfortunately they usually take place on grounds that weren't made for festivals. It also rains more over there, but they never cancel when that happens. And if the crowd doesn't like you, they pelt you with plastic water bottles filled with piss or mud, so you end up cleaning your whole backline before it goes in the cases.

The guys in Massive Attack told me they just did a festival in Turkey where the local stagehands were 60- and 70-year-old men who were actual sheepherders their whole lives. We're talking about handling delicate instruments, and they're dropping them like it was a rock in a well. So a summer festival tour in Europe is often your baptism by fire, and you just have to keep a cool head.

Do you have any advice for someone just starting out in the touring business?
Remember that the gig that you're working on today determines the gig that you'll be on tomorrow, because everybody's in the same network. The cooler you can be and the better the impression you make on your first tour, the better your chances will be that you'll see many more tours for the rest of your life. Maintain your composure at all times and never claim that you know it all. There's a time to ask questions, and there's a time to just stand there with elephant ears and listen. You'll get more accomplished by listening to the right people than you will by asking the wrong people the wrong questions.

Bob Glaub

Since the '70s, Bob Glaub has been a first-call bass player for superstars such as Stevie Nicks, Linda Ronstadt, Jackson Browne, Don Henley, John Fogerty, Bruce Springsteen, and many more. Currently on tour with the legendary Crosby, Stills, and Nash, Bob gives us the benefit of his 30-plus years of experience on the road.

What was your first road gig?

The first rock tour I did was with a band called the Mac Almond Band, and shortly after that I went on tour with Dave Mason. That was in '74 and '75. I played with him for a year and a half. We weren't on buses back then; we flew everywhere. We'd get up in the morning, get to an airport, and fly to the next gig. If the runs were real close, like 150 miles or so, we'd get into a couple of rental cars and drive. That was back in the days of commercial flying before all the screening that we have today. It was a lot cheaper to fly then, and you could time it so you could actually make your gig. That would be impossible today.

How much rehearsal time do you usually get before you go on tour?

That varies according to the act you're playing with. For this tour with CSN, we had six days of rehearsal booked. One of those was cancelled, and we didn't rehearse all that much on the remaining days, to be honest. Steven, Graham, and David have been together for 41 years now, so they know their material and just want to get the tour going. The first couple of gigs are almost like dress rehearsals.

That being said, a friend of mine in a fairly big band just finished rehearsing for a month before they left on tour, so it's all different.

Have you been out with CSN before?

Yeah, I worked with them in '87 and '88, when I did a couple of tours and a couple of albums with them. One was with Crosby, Stills, and Nash and the other was Crosby, Stills, Nash, and Young. I toured with them last year, too.

What are you taking on the road with you gear-wise?

I've got two new matching Ampeg SVT-VRs, which is a reissue of the old SVT. The cabinets I'm using are the 4 by 10 model (SVT-410HLF) that are like a half of a standard 8 by 10 SVT cabinet. One of those is a spare that's set up next to the one I use, so I have them both on stage.

Is that what you usually take on the road?

You know, I've used a lot of different gear over the years. This is kind of new setup. I got them last year and I'm using them again this year, and I'm really happy with them. The reissues sound pretty close to the old ones. I haven't had an opportunity to do a direct A/B comparison, but they sound pretty darn good.

I like vintage gear, but I don't take vintage amps on the road. I have friends who are "vintage snobs," that would never take anything other than the original item, but I don't find the need to go find a vintage SVT right now.

How about your bases?

Bass-wise it's pretty simple on this tour. It's always different with different people that I play with. I just use the ones that I think will sound good for the particular type of music I'm playing. With this band I'm using three Fender Precision basses: a 1959 P Bass, a 1965 P Bass, and a 1961 model that I hot-rodded in the '70s with active pickups. I also have one Lakeland bass, which, until recently, was my signature model with that company. It's basically a really nice P Bass copy. I have a couple of bass ukuleles [bukuleles], which is a new instrument made by Kohala Ukulele Company. Those are cool. I've also got a little acoustic guitar and a bukulele for my hotel room.

Aren't you worried about taking expensive vintage basses on the road with you?

It does worry me a little bit. I used to be more worried about taking my instruments on the road than I am now. A couple of basses have been sitting in their cases for almost 20 years, so it's kind of fun to be playing them again. They were made to be played and I'm happy to be playing them, so it's kind of cool to have them with me. I get the what-ifs every now about what could happen, but I don't let that bog me down too much.

Steven Stills played bass on the first couple of CSN albums, and he's a really good bass player. He really likes Fender P Basses, and it really makes him happy to see me playing one. I've tried playing my Lakelands out on the road last year, but he's just a lot happier when he sees me with a real P Bass.

Do you have your own tech for this tour?

I share one with Steven—the world-famous Chainsaw [Ricky LaPointe]. I've worked with him before in the '80s with Jackson Browne. He usually works for Bruce Springsteen or Billy Joel during the summer, so we're lucky to have him this year.

Are you on a bus, or are you doing fly dates?

We're on a bus. Tonight we do a show, then we'll get on the bus and do about a 250-mile drive that'll take about four or five hours. It's really comfy. I'm traveling with Graham, and there's only four of us. Each of the guys has their own bus, so there are three band buses and two crew buses.

We'll get to a place and have a hotel room just for the gig and for any days off. We have hotels all the time, so we don't live out of the bus. There are some days where we do back-to-back gigs where we only have the room for the night to just sleep in, so we'll check out before soundcheck in those cases.

How has touring changed from the time you started until today?

When I first started I was 19 years old, so it was sex, drugs, and rock 'n' roll. Now it's eat well, find places to play golf on the days off, and sleep a lot. [Laughs.] So that's changed quite a lot.

Has travel gotten any easier?

Yeah, it has gotten easier. Everything is so organized now. You have fabulous tour managers that give you a memo every day that tells you where to be and when, when you're soundchecking, when you're checking out, when your bags are supposed to be picked up, and when your meals are. Yeah, it's pretty easy. It's like summer camp for grownups. [Laughs.] Oh yeah, and by the way, we work. We do a gig about four or five times a week, so it's not all that hard.

We do have some pretty long trips over the next two weeks, and then when we get to Europe, there'll be some good drives between gigs as well. That makes catching up on sleep challenging. It doesn't really work to be on the road and go to bed early, when you're working from 8 to 10:30 every night and you have to be at your peak during that time. That means it doesn't really work for me to be an early bird.

Do you have any tips for staying healthy on the road?

Yeah—eat well, watch your diet, and exercise. I go to the gym at the hotels we stay at three or four days a week. You have to stay active and walk around the cities you visit, rather than sitting in your hotel room and being a vegetable.

How about packing to go on the road?

My girlfriend makes fun of me because I start thinking about packing two weeks before the tour. [Laughs.] Clothes are what they are. I bring some exercise clothes and some pretty low-key T-shirts to wear during the day, and a handful of shirts to wear for the gig. We're not really a very fancy-dressed band, so it's pretty low key as far as wardrobe is concerned. There is no wardrobe code, so you can just wear what you want, so that's not a challenge.

Packing stuff that I like to have around me is important. I like to take a laptop, a couple of books, some stereo speakers so I can listen to music from my laptop in the room, and an iPod for working out. Earplugs are really important. I've found that wax earplugs are really good for sleeping in hotels, because you won't hear the maids chatting in the hallway. I bring some mundane things like bills, because you have to still pay them even though you're on the road. That's why the computer is great, because it makes that so easy. We didn't have that in the old days. [Laughs.]

If you were going to hire a tech, what would you look for?

First of all, someone that I get along with, so hopefully our personalities will mesh. Someone who's technically knowledgeable enough to keep everything working, and someone who's in tune with the sounds I like. I'm not all that difficult to work for, because my setup is pretty basic and I don't use a lot of effects or anything—so somebody that I dig being around and is knowledgeable enough to do the job is what I'd look for.

What was the worst tour you ever did?

I've never really had one that I can remember. If I did, they were all great learning experiences, and there were always cool people to meet. There are ones that I didn't love as much as others, but they weren't that bad.

Mike Holmes

Mike Holmes is unique in that he's one of the few guys in Nashville that is known strictly for his piano and organ chops. Having started his touring career with the legendary Temptations, Mike later played with a host of Nashville's finest, include Lee Greenwood, Leroy Parnell, and Delbert McClinton, among many others. Mike has a lot of experience carrying a full B-3 on tour, and he's able to share some tips with us here.

What was your first road gig?

My first significant road gig was with the Temptations in 1980. There were two keyboard players on the gig. One of us played organic instruments (which, thankfully, was me), and the other keyboardist played synth parts with analog horn and string patches, which was the sound of the day back then.

How did your Hammond travel?

For that gig most of the travel was flying and the back and frontline gear was all rentals. After I came to Nashville, everything was on buses, though. Initially I had a pair of dollies and some packing blankets for the B-3, but later on I had flight cases made for everything, which your crew hates to see because it can double the weight of the gear.

For a while, the in-vogue thing here was to have cases built out of the same kind of fiber as drum cases. They weighed about a third as much as the road cases but they weren't as heavy duty, and you couldn't fly with them because they weren't ATA approved. But if you were traveling by land and you had a crew you could trust to handle everything the proper way, they worked pretty well and they did lighten the load a lot.

What kind of rehearsal did you have before you went out on the road?
For an extended tour, we'd have a week to ten days of rehearsals. That being said, a lot of the tours out of Nashville are what folks call a "hillbilly weekend." That's where you leave town on Thursday, play a show on Friday and Saturday and maybe Sunday, then come back home. There's not as much rehearsal in those cases.

What do you take on the road with you?
If the wherewithal is there to transport it, nowadays I always take a weighted key controller with some good piano samples, a B-3, and one Leslie 122 for sure. You just don't see many guys out on the road any more that actually carry a B-3 and a Leslie. Guys these days are thought of more as "keyboard" guys because there's so much sampling and sequencing going on, but I'm still one of the few "organic" keyboard guys. You can find some great Hammond organ samples and some great Leslie simulators, but it just doesn't sound the same. You have to move some air to get the real sound. It's funny, because in the late '70s and early '80s, you just could not give away a B-3. Guys started buying them for $500 or $600, and now they sell for ten times that amount.

I've also got a bunch of Wurlitzer 100As and 206s that I collect, but I'm reluctant to carry them on the road these days because it's so hard to get parts for them. I just bought some new tines for one of them, and they were 20 bucks a pop!

What do you take as backup?
I'll often take a couple of sound modules and keep them stashed just in case I need them. I don't carry a spare controller because I usually don't have a problem with it because it's so reliable.

Do you have a tech?
If it's a serious tour, of course. I'll usually share one with the guitar player or bass player, but there's always someone there to support you.

Do you have any audition tips?
I did some auditions in L.A. but I've never done any in Nashville, and I've

been here for 20 years. I always felt that if someone is auditioning players that he's not already aware of, it's a clue that he's looking for something else besides the way you play or the gear that you have. It's a good tip that they may be looking more at how you look or at your age. I've seen that a lot. So I don't do any auditions and I don't think it's kept me from getting any gigs, because the ones I get hire me because they want the way I play as opposed to wanting someone to play however the guy on the record played.

Do you have tips for being on the road?

Watch your diet. That's a big deal. I've seen so many guys that would go out on their first tour and come back a year later and they'd gained 40 pounds. You get to the venue at about four o'clock and backstage there's going to be catering, it's going to be good, and you're going to pig out. As you know, musicians are not known for their self-control.

So the ticket for me has always been a bicycle. I keep a mountain bike under the bus in the baggage compartment and that's what saves me. In the last 20 years, for me it's become a package deal—"No bike, no Mike." When the other guys are holed up in the hotel all afternoon, I'm out pedaling.

What do you usually pack to go on the road?

You have your civilian wear and you have your stage wear, and I would pack those separately. My civilian bag goes in and out of the hotel with me, and the stage bag stays on the bus because that's where everyone changes anyway, so it never leaves the bus.

Typically, I'll pack enough stage wear to cover three or four shows. For civilian wear, I'll take enough for about a week. That's all I'm going to take, so whatever else I'm taking has to fit in those two bags.

What do you take with you for entertainment?

Everyone here is used to doing the weekend tour thing, so I listen to a lot of music and it's a good outlet for me because I'll use that time to review what I've done in the studio that week. A lot of times I'll come back with ideas I didn't have before I left. It's a good kind of laboratory.

What's your soundcheck like? Is there anything that you try to work out?

If your crew is tight, then tonight's show should sound exactly like it did last night. Lee Greenwood's crew is a good example. You could uproot everything, travel 500 miles, and only need one song for the soundcheck and you're done. They were sharp enough to make it sound the same every time.

Sometimes when I have to share gear with the support act, I come on stage and listen to what the other keyboard player was listening to in the monitors and I don't understand how they can play. All they'll have in the monitor is them. I want to hear the whole band, because I'm there to play with everybody else. I don't understand how you can do that if you can't hear the guy across the stage from you.

Have you used in-ears?

Yeah, I've worked with them but I'm not a big fan, to tell you the truth. It sounds good, better than headphones in the studio, but it also sounds sort of sterile to me. You can't feel it. I'd just rather feel some air moving, because that's what my ears and my mind needs. Maybe it's just my demographic speaking here though. *[Laughs.]*

Do you ever use a real piano?

It's hard to tour with a real piano any more because it's so easy just to take a weighted controller, but we both know that they're not there yet when compared to a real piano. I am a big fan of the Yamaha Motif. The sounds speak for themselves, but I think since Yamaha makes great acoustic pianos, they actually think about the action more than other manufacturers. You get the idea that whoever created the action on the Motif thought to themselves that they might have to play it themselves one day.

What was you worst road experience?

I went to Sicily with Solomon Burke, and the airline between Nashville and New York lost my luggage, so I ended up in Sicily in August with no clothes. The Italians pretty much take the whole month of August off, so all the shops where closed and I had to wear what I had on for about a week. Solomon offered to let me wear a couple of his outfits but he weighs about 400 pounds and I only weigh 180, so that wasn't going to work. I realize that if that's your worst story, then you probably have had a pretty trouble-free career. *[Laughs.]*

What was you best?

At the end of the Temps tour, our last show was at the Greek Theater in L.A. I had only been to L.A. a couple of times, but I had a lot friends there. After the show, I met Solomon backstage for the first time, and he told me how much he liked my playing. He said, "Where do you live?" and I told him I was from Birmingham Alabama. He said, "Have you ever thought about moving to L.A,?" and so I took that as a cue and stayed. It was the beginning of a whole new chapter in my life. I stayed for almost ten years before I moved to Nashville.

Terry Lawless

Terry Lawless is one of the premier keyboard techs on the road today, having spent the past nine years with superstar band U2. It's not the only elite act that has utilized Terry's expertise, though; he's also been out with Don Henley, the Doobie Brothers, Bruce Springsteen, Cher, Phil Collins, and David Bowie, among others. Terry is also a great keyboard player himself, and you can find more information about him at www.terrylawless.com. A fountain of useful information, Terry has an abundance of useful tips and tricks thanks to his many years of road experience.

What was your first road gig?
The first one that anyone would know was with Barry Manilow back in 1986. I was a keyboard and guitar tech, plus I ended up playing some bit parts in the show as a background singer and utility dancer. I also set up his grand piano and kept it in tune. I was kind of a jack-of-all-trades on that one.

Are you a piano tuner yourself?
I am, but I'm so slow at it that I wouldn't call myself a tuner. If a tuner doesn't show up, I'll tune our CP-80 [an early electro-acoustic piano made by Yamaha] myself, but I'm a lot slower than a real pro. It's a good skill to have, though.

How did you get the Manilow gig?

As with most gigs, it's a recommendation from someone else. The fellow that had the gig before me was getting promoted up into the band. I knew him from living in the San Fernando Valley [part of Los Angeles] and running into him all the time as a player and as a tech, so he knew I could handle the MIDI end of it and sent the gig to me.

What are your responsibilities as a keyboard tech?

When you're working as a keyboard tech, you're in charge of maintaining and setting up the keyboard systems and making sure they work the same every day. If there are any programming needs, you have to be able to program whatever sounds the player wants. Sometimes you have to set up splits on the keyboard, which means you have to be able to think musically, too, like in the case where you know enough to program a sample in a certain spot on a keyboard so that it won't bother the rest of the player's performance.

I've seen a lot of techs come and go, and they're usually let go for, let's say, "bad habits" or for a problem in the rig that becomes a recurring problem. If at a certain point in the show every night the player is more concerned about whether the gear will work than about making music, that usually means the tech won't stay on the job too long. The prime directive for us is to make it so the player does not have to worry about anything else except making music, and to make it exactly the same for them every day so that they can just step up on stage and step into their slot.

Then it breaks down into smaller things than that, like packaging everything right so it travels well and tracing down hums and buzzes. If there are problems with the performance of certain patches, you have to be able to adjust those kinds of parameters. A player might say, "I'd really like to have this so I can get the same sound with a lighter touch," and you have to be able to do that for him quickly. You really have to know the technical end, because over the last 20 years, as things got more technical, it became kind of a split-mind kind of thing for a player, where you had to learn either the technical end or the musical end of things. It was difficult to spend enough time on both and know both well, so the player relies upon you to understand the technical end so they can pursue the musical end.

From the crew point of view, it's being a participant in everything from load-in to load-out, knowing the ins and outs of truck packing so everything rides safely so you don't spend your time repairing things on the other end, and knowing all the bench-tech techniques, from something as simple as soldering to something as difficult as tracing down breaks in a circuit board. It's all different levels of knowledge at that point, but the more you bring to the table, the more you're going to work.

Tell me a bit more about programming.

A common thing for many groups is that they want to sound just like their records, but you have to do it on whatever equipment they decide they're going to take out. That means you might have to get a Korg Trinity sound from something like a Roland G-8, so you need programming chops on a number of synths.

When you first started, everything was very MIDI-centric, and now it's all computer-centric. Does that make it easier for you, or more difficult?

I've been doing this for a long time, so I never noticed the transition that much. I grew up with MIDI, and I was there at the beginning of synthesizer programming when the Prophet 5 (the first programmable synthesizer) first came out and not many people understood what was going on. When computers started to take over, I was right there programming sequences from maybe the late '80s or so, even if it was only for sound effects or for a click track (since you have to lock to video sometimes). Simple became complex, but it really wasn't like a big tidal wave, it was more gradual. I was working a lot then, so I just absorbed as much as I could so it wasn't really a rush. One thing kind of streamed into the other as a natural progression, so the guys that got in on it in the beginning were the ones that better understood it.

How much is really centered around the computer now?

In the last 20 years, practically every show is centered around the computer in one way or another. Having a computer that locks the band up to lighting cues or video cues suddenly fell in the lap of the keyboard player or the keyboard player's tech, and no one ever questioned that.

Using computers in keyboard systems came into vogue, but there are definite problems with putting a computer up on stage. The reboot time is too long if it goes down [who's never had a computer that's crashed on them at the wrong time?], and a little thing like having this shinning screen there during a complete blackout cue on stage was unacceptable. It just couldn't happen anymore, so we had to go to alternative methods. The Muse Research Receptor allowed you to run VST instruments on stage without a computer, so it's now a standard just for that reason. You don't see computers as much as you did about six or seven years ago, because the computer on stage was impractical.

The last time I ran a keyboard system with a computer on stage was with Paul Mirkovich on the Cher tour so he could run a grand piano and a virtual organ. Most of her stuff was based on hardware synths anyway, but a really good piano and a really good Hammond organ was done virtually. We actually ran the computer back by me and triggered it via MIDI from his station, but at that time you'd see a lot of musicians that would put a laptop up on stage with them. That wasn't received well by the audience. They thought that there was a lot that it was controlling, because immediately when people see a computer they think, "Sampled vocals." The problems we had in the '90s with computers really put the kibosh on using them after the turn of the century.

Does that mean that any backing tracks that might be used come from the keyboard player or the keyboard tech?

Yes, if they're being used, and to tell you the truth I see them used quite a bit out on the road. They're usually triggered by the keyboard tech. Very rarely will they put them up with the keyboard player, mostly because they don't want to draw any attention to it. In my career I've run a lot of backing tracks, but it just doesn't seem right. There are certain little sound effects and drum loops and things like that that enhance a performance. But there are still people that will overdo it just because they can. That seems to be going away, though.

The problem was worse back in the early '80s when MTV hit. Everyone wanted the band to sound and look just like they did on MTV. That was a big part of it back then.

What do you take out with you in your workbox?

We're lucky enough to have a bench tech on our crew, but when I'm going out myself as a keyboard tech, I take a laptop because there are a lot of programs for MIDI analysis or libraries that come in handy. I'll take some rudimentary tools. You have to make sure that you have a spare internal battery for every piece of gear that you have, a complement of short to long audio cables, some really long MIDI cables (up to 50 feet; it really doesn't matter if they're short or long, because they'll work fine), cleaners for the keys and tops of keyboards, and some extra lightbulbs.

In my workbox I also carry a really good soldering station, because bad soldering jobs are as good as no soldering jobs sometimes. I keep a spare MIDI and a spare USB keyboard around, a headphone amp for troubleshooting, a good pair of isolated headphones so that you can hear no matter what level the band is playing on stage, and an assortment of hand tools, because you have to crack the chest of a keyboard quite a bit. If you're on a show that uses a predominance of Roland keyboards, you try to carry an extra set of Roland keys—both weighted and unweighted. You carry extra power cords. You carry a supply of every battery that you're going to need in the show, because why would you put a half-a-million-dollar show on the line for a 99-cent battery?

I also carry an assortment of regular wireless and MIDI wireless systems as well as some MIDI long-transmission gadgets that will let you send MIDI to the front of house if you need to. I carry the manual for every item that I take on the road. If you're carrying something unique like a Fender Rhodes piano, you have to carry parts and tines for that. If you're keeping a Hammond organ running, it's a good idea to keep a spare Leslie around. If you can't, you need to keep a full assortment of tubes, belts, and O-rings. In my workbox, because I've gotten a name as a Hammond person, I carry a Trek Hammond preamp that will accept any pinnage of cable out of the back. I also keep a Variac in my workbox just in case the voltage gets weird, so you can bump the voltage up or down as necessary if you don't have an electrician on hand. That's one of the staples of my workbox.

You try to have a spare for everything that you have on stage, and if that's not possible, you have one generic keyboard crammed with every program that you use in the show just so you can slide it in as a replacement for any keyboard up there.

You carry a lot of space blankets and plastic sheeting that you can toss up at anytime. One of the most important things that you can carry in your workbox is a hair dryer. We built a unit out of a piece of PVC pipe that you can mount a hair dryer to that has holes drilled in it. You can then mount it over a keyboard just to have some warm air blowing out there. Sometimes it's good to keep a big pop-up umbrella in the truck.

After you set up a show and have everything working, you go through a series of what-ifs. You go through every piece of gear and say to yourself, "What if this goes down?" This is very important—when you back up programs on a synthesizer, you have to do it on at least two different media. You may have them backed up on your computer, but what if your computer goes down? You may have them backed up on a MIDI data filer with a floppy disk, but what if that goes down? Whenever possible, you have everything backed up on RAM cards because that's the fastest thing you can use to restore everything. The important thing is to have backups of your backups in different media if possible, just so you can cover you self.

You also take a multimeter so you can meter the power before you plug in, because sometimes it's not right. Even the simplest little three-pronged polarity tester will tell you whether things are wired correctly. That's a ten-second test that can save you thousands of dollars.

What's the most difficult thing you have to do?
The most difficult thing is making sure everything is the same on stage every day, regardless of the situation you're in. Depending upon the size of the act, the bigger the stage, the more you're going to be able to make it the same every show. The most difficult thing is working with a smaller act in smaller venues and still trying to make it feel the same and be comfortable for the player. You just have to get creative about it sometimes.

Other than that, the hardest thing for any tech to get down is the hang, because the hang will make or break you in the business. You have to be able to work with other people and do your own work without stepping on anybody's toes and making them upset. That's what the whole touring world relies on, and that's why it's mostly the same people doing most of the jobs, because people that don't fit in get weeded out quickly, and people that work well with other people get asked back.

Is there a certain type of venue that you don't like?
I don't like being outdoors, because the weather's so variable. That's the most difficult challenge: compensating for weather and trying to keep the instruments playable and protected at the same time. You have dust or water, or cold or heat. Instruments have a heat tolerance, and if you go on either side of it, they just shut down so you have to find some ways around that.

Do you have a maintenance schedule on the gear, or do you just fix it when it breaks?
If you take the time to put everything in their cases carefully and keep them clean and maintained when they're on stage, you don't have to do that other part. It's preventative maintenance more than it's maintenance by taking care of it today so you don't have to fix it tomorrow.

One of the things that keep me working is that I do as much of everything as I can myself, because I know how I want it handled. There's a whole method of working with stagehands to tell them, "Let's grab it from this leg and with this hand under the front and we'll lay it on its back, lifting it so there's no pressure on the legs." Just taking five seconds to say that is worth the 20 minutes that it might take to fix it the next day.

One of the other things that's always been pretty good for me is that I'm always respectful to stagehands, and you don't always see that. Stagehands will work very well with you and will be very careful when you ask them to, if you treat them like the human beings that they are. That's been one of the keys to my success. I work well with stagehands because I treat them well.

What should a player look for in a tech?

Usually a player looks for someone who can handle his particular technical side, but you want to find someone that will do it in a musical way. A player doesn't want to have to ask you to do something another way because what you did doesn't work smoothly during the performance. If you can find someone who's musical enough to understand that, and make it so you can just walk in and easily understand how what he did works in performance, that's what you want. They have to know what parts you're playing, what key you're playing them in, and when you're using different instruments and how you're using them. A player is always going to look for someone that brings more to the table than the next guy.

It's a fine line, because you really want someone who's going to handle the technical problems from a musical point of view, but you want someone who will just step back and get out of your way when you're playing.

Which brings me to another point that's a well-understood rule of the road. As a tech, you want to let the player know that you know a lot about what you're doing without coming off like a player. They'll feel comfortable if they know you can play some, but you never say that. That's a cardinal sin. I know a lot of techs that don't work, just because they come off too much like a player and not enough like a tech. It happens quite often actually.

How do you stay healthy on the road?

The first thing is to eat healthy. The second thing is to stay away from bad vices. The third thing is to get enough sleep. After a show, instead of sitting up and knocking down a dozen beers and watching movies, you should just go to bed because you need to rest to do your job well. You have to understand when it's a school night and what you need to do to stay sharp the next day. On your days off, you should get out and walk or exercise.

The most important thing is to eat healthy, and it's so easy not to in our situation. There are snacks and sodas around all day, and you have a number of choices for meals because most tours are very well catered. So you need to watch your diet and keep your weight down. A lot of guys put on weight when they go out on tour because they eat a lot at meals and eat a lot after the show.

What do you take for entertainment?

I still listen to a lot of music, although I couldn't for a long time and then I rediscovered it again. I read a lot and have had a Kindle for a long time. I also have a little DAW system that I can take to the hotel room so I can work on recording, and that takes up a lot of my time and keeps my programming and playing chops up.

When you're packing for a tour, is there something that you always have to take with you?

Most of the time when we pack, it's seven pairs of black jeans and seven black shirts, and maybe a couple of shirts for days off. Make sure that you can get from laundry to laundry, because there's nothing worse than wearing dirty clothes. I like to have new socks whenever I can, so I'm always buying new socks. You have to have backups in your personal life just like in your professional one. I have backups of shampoos, toothpaste, and things like that because there's nothing worse than getting stuck in a hotel six miles outside of town and not have anything to wash you hair with.

In my workbox I always have a change of gig clothes and a change of day-off clothes that are always clean and sealed away. I keep another pair of shoes in my workbox, because sometimes you'll get your shoes sopping wet out in the rain and then you'll have to do a show with wet feet, which is awful. I keep a raincoat and a hooded sweatshirt in there, too, so you can dress in layers and can keep yourself warm even if all you brought was a light jacket. It's a good idea to take a pair of long underwear if you're touring the northeastern U.S. in the winter, because you never know when you might have to go and dig out a truck that's stuck in snow.

Again, you just start with your what-ifs. Keep an extra set of sunglasses, some sunscreen, and some insect repellant. Everybody on the road knows that Avon Skin So Soft is one of the best insect repellants that you'll ever find. Everybody always has a bottle of Gold Bond powder in their suitcase. It's a balance of traveling light and making sure that you can get from laundry to laundry. On most touring stops these days, you can leave a laundry bag and pick it up after the show that night, so you don't have to do your own laundry anymore. I always carry incense for the stinky rooms that you sometimes get. I keep a flashlight in case the hotel power goes off, and you never know when you'll need a camera.

Has touring changed from the time you started?

The biggest thing that's changed is the availability of tickets for shows, which doesn't happen any more. They realized how much they were giving away, so there just aren't many comped tickets anymore. Salaries have gone up considerably, which is good if you have to buy your own tickets.

Right around the end of the '90s, touring really became more corporate and seemed to be taken over by accountants. Since I started, I'd have to say that it's a lot cleaner business that it used to be. There isn't as much alcohol and drug abuse around at the upper levels. And the accommodations get better as the acts you work with get bigger.

What was the worst gig you ever did?

I worked for an artist that was really set in his ways and really wanted to run everything from the stage rather than hiring people he trusted and just letting them do their job. As an example, the last truck we had was filled with metal detectors that went around all the entrances of the arena. I had to ask myself, "Why am I working for someone that needs metal detectors on the entrances?" I only did two shows with him.

What was the best?

The job that I have right now is great and I can't say enough about that, but the most inspiring man I ever worked for was David Bowie. He was a workaholic and tremendous at whatever he attempted to do, whether it was painting, sculpting, writing, music, or poetry. He probably could have been a finish carpenter if he wanted to. He was a complete pro the whole time and had that thing that when he was on stage you couldn't take your eyes off him. If I had to single out a person, he would be it. My boy's named Bowie, which is a tribute to the effect that one man had on me. Still to this day, just the mention of his name makes me inspired to go out and do something.

If I had to single out a band, I'd have to say that U2 is the best job that you could ever want. The guys are tremendous, not only as musicians but as human beings. They are four of the greatest human beings that I've ever met.

Heather Lockie

Heather Lockie is a violist who loves to play with a loose federation of female string players known appropriately as "Rock 'n' Roll Strings," the players of which have worked with a number of well-known artists such as Spiritualized, Eels, Dave Matthews, Linda Ronstadt, Brian Wilson, Wilco, and many more. Heather's a bit different from most string players in that she comes more from a rock and experimental background rather than classical, which makes her take about life on the road even more interesting, since she's lived the musical life of an artist as well as a support musician. You can see more on the Rock 'n' Roll Strings at www.myspace.com/rocknrollstringslosangeles.

I found you through your MySpace page. Is that how you get a lot of your work?

I just made that MySpace page because we had some photos that we thought were awesome, and thought it would be a good idea to have a page to be able to refer people to. [Laughs.] As far as work goes, I don't know if I divine where work is at or if work divines where I'm at, but it just seems to happen. A lot of it's word of mouth, and a lot of it is people you know.

What was the first tour?

I toured many times with my own bands (Leather Hyman and Listing

Ship) since the mid-'90s. Between those bands, I went on the road maybe nine or ten times. Then I went out with Arthur Lee and Love, and eventually with Spiritualized, and then the Eels a few times. I've been on tour with tons of indie bands that you've probably never heard of, so I've had two different touring lives. On an independent tour, it's like, "Where are we going to sleep tonight?" But then on a bigger tour, you're staying in four-star hotels, playing larger venues, and getting a per diem. They're totally different worlds and they're both really valuable experiences.

Most string players don't seem to travel in that indie world.
There are many different kinds of string players. I'm different in that I had a somewhat formal education where I took lessons growing up and was in a public school system that had a music program, but I didn't study it intensively in undergrad. All the while, I was playing music, but I didn't learn to improvise until I was 18, and it took me about two years to get a grip on what that was. I was just playing really badly with a lot of records and a lot of people trying to figure out how to access that part of the brain, because it's so different than reading music. Then I started writing my own songs with my band partner Lyman Chaffee, and that became the majority of my small-band touring experience. But since I've done some of the larger tours, I've met so many different kinds of string players.

There's a small percentage of string players that can bridge the classical and the improvisational world, and there's an even smaller percentage that can do both of those things well. I'm really lucky to have played with some of the musicians that I've worked with in the last five years, because they're just so incredible. But we have the same kind of problems as other musicians in regards to personalities and substances sometimes. For the most part, most of the professionals are really together because you have to be, especially if you're going to be a support musician.

How big is the section that you go out with?
For the most part, the strings would be a quartet, and even a quintet, but there might be additional horn or woodwind players, too.

Do you take your main instrument with you, or do you have one that's specifically for touring?
I have a backup that doesn't play as well as my main instrument, but it's much cheaper to replace. [Laughs.] When I'm going on a bigger tour, I take my main instrument, because the security is better and I'm not as

afraid of something bad happening. But I make sure to take the viola with me almost everywhere, unless it's behind a locked door or on a secure backstage.

What kind of case do you use? Do you have a road case for it?

A good instrument case will protect it pretty well, so that's what I use. It's just a normal classical-instrument case. It's very hot to have a BAM case, because they're so lightweight and yet supposedly can fall from an airplane to the ground and keep the instrument safe . . . but if you are in that plane, you're probably not going to care much.

What about flying?

If you're anal about it, you detune the strings, but it's usually fine if you don't. I just put a humidifier strip in the case to keep it humidified. It's not so much the cold that will affect the instrument—it's the heat. Extreme heat can make the glue melt, but that's usually not an issue with flying.

I always carry my instrument on with me. Jessica Catron, whom I've been on a couple of tours with, is required to buy a plane ticket for her cello so it can be on the seat beside her, so the people that hire her have to account for that. She won't check it, and it's too big to put in the overhead bin. You can fit a viola in the overhead, though, so there's usually not any big issues.

Right after 9/11, people got really funny about me bringing my viola on board. They didn't know what rosin was, which caused a bit of a problem. Once I was taken back behind the security station, where they questioned me pretty heavily about the rosin. [Laughs.] I told them, "It's not hash, even though it looks like it. It's for my bow, and players need it to make a sound from their instruments." Then they got it and let me go. I haven't had that problem since.

What do you bring for backups?

I bring a couple of bows. In terms of pedals, I can bring a small suitcase with effects pedals if they're needed. I'll take a volume pedal, wah pedal, distortion, delay, and various other pedals. Most of the string players I play with are really adept at making those kinds of sounds and doing experimental stuff. There are pieces out there for amplified strings where you're expected to run through different pedals, so you have to have them. Sometimes they want a straight string sound, but a lot of the independent bands want different kinds of sounds and you're free to experiment.

How is your viola miked? Do you have your own setup, or do you rely on the sound company?

I used to have an L. R. Baggs pickup, which was pretty good, but now I have this pretty amazing pickup called a Shertler. The frequency response is really even, but you have to have it installed in your bridge. It's a great-sounding pickup.

What's the onstage monitoring like for a string player?

Monitoring is a big issue for strings. If you're playing with a loud rock band, they don't have any conception of what it's like to play a fretless instrument, where you have to hear not only yourself, but the main guitar and bass so you can blend with those instruments. Also, it helps to hear the other string players. There's a different sound that comes from a bowed instrument that blends in the aural space much differently than a plectoral instrument.

Do you listen to wedges, or do you have in-ears?

In-ears proved to be better for me when we toured with the Eels, because the band was so loud on stage. We actually considered putting up a Plexiglass block, but that proved impossible for every show. So the second time we went out, we got in-ears and it was much better. The in-ears also protect you against stage volume.

What do you have to hear in your mix?

We really have to hear the things that are the least tunable in themselves, like a piano or a keyboard, because they have a set tuning. We can modify our tuning to match it if we can hear it.

Did you have to audition for any of your road gigs?

Mostly I got these gigs without auditions. The people that hire us in general want to play with people that can problem-solve, be dependable, and be able to deal with all the personalities as well as play the part. If you're too much of a personality yourself, you might have difficulties. That's just purely from a support musician's standpoint. I'm not saying that you shouldn't have your own personality or opinions or wants and desires, but you have to be flexible and easygoing enough to understand that the gig is not about you—it's just about creating a vibe—and the individual doesn't matter so much.

How much rehearsal do you usually get before you go out on tour?

It really varies. It's a week or so on average, although sometimes it may go as long as a couple of weeks. Sometimes they'd be lockouts, and sometimes they'd be three-hour union blocks. It all depends on the budget.

Does that mean you're on a union gig when you go out?

That also depends. I've done both, and prefer the union gigs. I think they kind of balance out, though. Many bands/artists will hire outside of the union, and there is a fine line in terms of getting paid what you feel your time is worth and negotiating yourself out of the job. It's like communicating with spirits, gauging how much someone is willing to pay versus how much you're willing to not get paid. Some tours I've been on paid similarly to union scale but weren't union gigs. I'd get cash under the table, and the people funding the tour still got what they considered a good deal. Don't get me wrong—there are valuable aspects to being in a union and doing union gigs. They protect musicians to a degree and make sure you get paid appropriately, but if you stick to doing only union gigs, you may limit yourself to only half the gigs available.

If it's not a union gig, how do you set your rate?

One helpful way to approach negotiating pay might be to decide what your personal minimum pay would be. What's the least amount of money that you'd leave all your own projects for to go do this job? Conversely, what's your "ideal" rate of pay? Some advocate upping your ideal rate of pay by a third when you begin negotiating with an employer, and then feeling out how that is for the employer. If you're clear with yourself about your minimum rate for the job, then this process is painless and even kind of fun.

Also, artistically, you have to be clear about how you feel about the project, especially with independent projects where the artists are paying you out of their own pockets. Sometimes I'll play music for very little if I like the project and the music. On the other hand, there are projects that I just don't want my name on, like this one guy who wanted me to put viola on a soulful folk track that he had written, where one line references a dog farting by a fireplace. That's not so interesting to me, and I probably wouldn't have felt like it was a good use of my time if I had taken that job.

A word about per diems: you can make quite a bit more money if you don't actually spend your per diem. Many touring musicians I know save that money, eat simply and prudently on tour, and end up with a lot more money in their pockets at the end of it.

What do you personally pack when you go on the road?

Again, that really depends. Sometimes people want us to look like a classical quartet, in which case we bring generic fancy black attire that would blend into a stage. Sometimes they want us to wear costumes or outfits. I usually pack medium-light and take three or four outfits that go with each other so they can become more than three or four outfits. I'm not a really great packer. I'm more scattershot about it. I have friends who throw out socks and underwear and buy them as needed instead of doing laundry, but I'm not really into doing that.

Do you have any tips for staying healthy?

Yeah, get enough sleep and don't drink more than one or two cocktails a night if you can help it. *[Laughs.]* Take lots of vitamins. Resist the temptation to party all night. Just use some basic common sense.

One tip that I have is the way I deal with jet lag. I'd wake up at like four or five in the morning and go jogging. It's hard because your body is really tired, but if you can get yourself up and moving and get your circulation going, you can see a bit of the town you're in as well as help yourself adjust to the new time much more quickly than normal. That kind of exercise really energizes you, so you're more capable of dealing with the jet lag.

What do you take with you to entertain yourself on the bus?

A laptop, some books, lots of music. The first Eels tour came along at a really strange time. I was about to put out a record with my band Marshweed in L.A., and I felt kind of guilty about leaving and abandoning my own project. My band said it was okay, but the only way I could rationalize it within myself was to get a little recording setup that I would take with me and work on new material, because you have quite a bit of downtime during a tour.

Every time we'd reach a new venue, I set up my little Mbox recording studio; [I ended up working] on a series of eight or nine songs during the course of the tour. It was very productive, since there's at least three hours between the soundcheck and show where you're waiting around the venue.

What was the worst tour you've ever been on?

I don't think I've ever been on a horrific tour. I can say that the best and the most fun one with the lowest amount of drama was going out with Spiritualized. They're such kind and gentle people, who are really fun and don't mind partying with the support musicians, and not everyone is like that. Some stars are different in that respect. They're very private or they've been damaged by being in the public eye, which I can totally understand. It's a strange thing to be recognized wherever you go. But the guys in Spiritualized were very down with hanging out and going shopping and going to bars after the show. They were just wonderful people.

Arthur Lee was extremely gentlemanly. He was more removed from the support musicians, but he was very respectful and wonderful. He would greet us at the beginning of the show and shake everyone's hand and thank them at the end.

I have had some different issues on different tours, mostly with people not understanding that women can plug in a ¼-inch cable just as well as men can. There's a fair amount of sexism sometimes that's underlying in much of the touring industry.

As an example, I was in a rehearsal for a tour that shall remain nameless and there was a terrible blast of feedback. One of the string players unplugged her instrument and it happened to be up in the P.A. and made a loud pop. That led the sound guy to start with the "They don't understand how amplification works" line. That's automatically what they assumed. They were all really nice guys and trying hard to accommodate us, but I heard him say to the stagehand that was helping us out, "Make sure to unplug their instruments for them at the end of the rehearsal." We were like, "No, no, no! We know how this all works. We know what will happen. That was just an accident. Really, we're intelligent and it's not rocket science." From that point on, it wasn't a problem. It was just this basic assumption of, "We better do this for them because they can't."

That being said, what's the dynamic on the bus like for you?
It really depends upon the person that's controlling the money. If they're cool and reasonable and not damaged, then it's really fun. [Laughs.] If they're damaged or have women issues, then it can go from mildly uncomfortable to just weird. And it's all very subliminal, so sometimes there's nothing that you can really put your finger on.

Do you guys ever have your own tech, or do you share one with the guitar player?
It really depends upon the tour. On the small tours, I do everything myself. On the bigger tours, there's usually one or two of the other techs helping us out. I've never been on a tour where we've had our own string tech.

Michael McConnell

Michael McConnell began touring in an era when you pretty much did everything, from setting up the entire backline, mixing the sound, doing the stage managing, and taking care of anything else that would come up. From working as a guitar tech for Mick Jones of Foreigner, Glenn Tipton and Ian Hill of Judas Priest, Aldo Nova, and Foghat to tour managing/production managing and mixing front of house for Taylor Dayne, Joss Stone, and Billy Squier, among many others, Michael has seen it all and lived to tell us about it.

What are the typical duties of a guitar tech?

The first thing you do in the morning when the trucks are unloading is to separate the guitar trunks and your workbox, and send them to the tuning room.

In the tuning room you'll work on the guitars until it's time for the amps and cabinets to hit the stage. The number of guitars that you're responsible for will determine how long you spend in that room. For instance, with Judas Priest I took care of Glenn Tipton [one of the guitar players] and Ian Hill [the bass player]. Ian had three basses, but one was pretty much the only bass he used all night long and that one was restrung every day.

Tipton carried 11 guitars, of which 6 or 7 would be used during the show. The strings got changed about every third show. The guitars were all in a rotation, so there was fresh strings on one of the guitars every day but each guitar had its strings changed every third show.

When I worked with Mick Jones, he carried only three guitars [all Les Pauls], although I think he carries more than that now. One was his main guitar, another was for if he broke a string, and the third was a backup that he didn't care about too much. His main guitar only had the strings changed maybe once a week, because he didn't like new strings on his guitar. So with Mick, the gig wasn't as rigorous. You checked the setup of the guitars every day and cleaned them up, but you didn't have to change the strings every day.

Tipton and Hill was a lot bigger job. It took hours of work every day just to set up the guitars, then when you went to set up their rigs, it was even more work. They're a bit higher maintenance for a guitar tech than someone like Mick Jones. It's safe to say that if you teched for someone like Eddie Van Halen or Steve Vai, your job would be a lot more intense than if you were taking care of Mick Jones or somebody like that.

So back to the guitar room—the first thing I would do is pull out the main guitar. Every guitar player has a main guitar and that's the one that I would work on first because if there are any problems, you want to make sure you have enough time to get through it. I would clean it and check the setup and restring it if needed. After that I would stretch the strings, which might take a half hour of playing it and pulling the strings, then move on to the next one. That's what you've got to do every day you've got a show. God forbid if something major went wrong, so you're not having to be in your hotel room doing a repair job on your day off. I've heard of techs doing entire fret jobs on a day off.

When the cabinets hit the stage, it's time to go set the rigs up. If you have a guitarist like Tipton that uses four Marshal heads and bottoms, then you have to get those set up. If they have a rack, then you have to set it up and get it going and then make sure everything works.

What kind of gear did you bring with you?
Every tech has tools that will handle anything—a whole slew of Allen keys, a whole slew of wrenches, wrenches to handle Floyd Roses, Allen keys specific to certain manufacturer's parts, screwdrivers, files, nut stock, bridge saddles, and you have to have a soldering iron. You can't carry everything, but you can certainly carry enough to fix something quickly. For the amps, I would carry spare tubes, but I've seen techs that were boffins who even carry extra capacitors and transformers in some cases. With Priest we would carry several complete sets of tubes. With other acts we would carry one or two full sets. If a guitar player has 6 leads in his system, you'd

carry twice as many cables as you used, so you'd take 12 out with you. Some bands aren't able to bring as many spares because of finances, so you have to be prepared to be fixing stuff all the time.

A lot of what you end up carrying will always depend upon the act that you're with. When you're in rehearsals, you put together a kit of spares for whatever gear you're using. With one act we carried a plethora of wah-wah pedals because the guitar player abused them. Rather than carrying the components for the pedal and just keep on working on the same one, we would carry three or four and just cycle them. The gear takes a beating, so you have to carry spares of all kinds of stuff. And as you know, a lot of the gear that's sitting on stage is backup and is not normally being used. Glen Tipton had four heads on stage, but only one was ever used and the other three were backups.

What types of gigs are the hardest?

Generally, the bigger the venue, the easier the gig. The easiest gigs to do are arenas and stadiums. Stadiums aren't as comfortable, because they're outside and it presents a whole other slew of potential issues, like working on a guitar in an air-conditioned room, then taking it outside in 100-degree weather. For those types of gigs, you generally end up working outside, which is uncomfortable for you but better for the instruments. So arenas, casinos, and even some theaters are good gigs because they're all roomy and temperature is controlled.

As the venues start getting smaller, the tougher the gig gets. Old theaters and clubs are completely horrible because generally you don't have much room or a place to work on the instruments, and there are always issues with temperature. Clubs always seem to be freezing, or hot, or both. You'll have some bad things happen, like someone will open a door and you'll get a blast of 30-degree temperature right where your guitars are sitting because there's no where else to set up. Bands like these gigs because they're more intimate, but the crew usually hates them.

What's different in touring between now and when you started?

It's become very corporate these days. Today everything is pretty strictly business; back then it was a lot looser. I don't mean it was unprofessional, but you had a lot more freedom in how to get something accomplished. Now you're touring with a tour accountant who's watching every penny and it's all business. And loyalty was a big factor back then. If you worked with a band and they liked you, they stayed loyal to you. Now, they are less likely to have any loyalty towards you. If you're not willing to work for the amount that you're offered, you don't work. It's not the artist, it's the business that's taken over, and it's a whole different vibe as a result. To me, everything started changing in the beginning of the '90s, and it's made it a much more sterile environment today.

That being said, from a technological standpoint, everything is much better now. The gear is better and more reliable, and everything is sonically so much better now on most tours these days.

How do you stay healthy on the road?

In terms of food, you can eat pretty healthy these days because you don't have to eat junk. For some artists, healthy food is definitely a prerequisite. If you're touring with McCartney, you may be eating vegan but you're eating good food. Other artists carry their own catering. When you do European tours, you always carry your own catering so you can eat whatever you want. So all that "You can't eat right on the road stuff" is crap. You can even pull into a truck stop and get a salad or something decent to eat these days. It doesn't have to be greasy hamburgers and french fries. That's just fast and easy.

What is the best tour you've ever been on?

I've had several bests. Joss Stone was a favorite, and Mellancamp was great musically. Joss Stone because on top of being incredibly talented, she is one of the sweetest human beings I've ever met. It made every day really pleasant. But there hasn't been one tour that I went, "God, this is so incredible," while it was happening, except maybe Squier.

What should a guitar player look for in a tech?

Based on my experiences, it's based more on personality than anything else. For most players, it's really important to find someone they like and can get along with. That being said, some players just want an "A-list guy," meaning someone with experience working for U2 or Sting or Aerosmith or someone like that. Everybody always assumes that if you've worked for those kinds of bands that you're the best, but I've come to learn that that's not always the case. Most of those guys are really good or they wouldn't be in that position in the first place, but it's never a sure thing. A recommendation from someone that they really respect carries a ton of weight as well.

Is there anything that you always take on tour with you?

Nowadays it's a laptop. That's become a tool that's hard to be without, because it's 50 percent for work and 50 percent for entertainment. I have no idea how I toured before laptops and cell phones. I really have no clue.

Paul Mirkovich

Paul Mirkovich is arguably one of the highest-profile keyboardists on the planet. As musical director and keyboard player for the television shows *Rock Star: INXS* and *Rock Star: SuperNova*, Paul has been seen by millions of television viewers. But Paul has spent plenty of time on the road as well, having been the musical director for Cher, Pink, Janet Jackson and Anastasia as well as touring with Whitesnake, Jeffery Osbourne and Paul Stanley (of Kiss), among many others. Paul's the perfect guy to give us some insight as to what it's like being an MD for a major artist.

I know that your first road gig was with Jeffery Osbourne. What kind of gear were you playing then?

For the first couple of tours, I played the second keyboard chair and I used most of the things that were popular at the time. I think I had a Jupiter 8, a DX-7, some DX-7 rackmounted modules, and maybe an Oberheim OB-8 as well.

Keyboard tech Terry Lawless told me that he teched for you on a Cher tour and that you had a fairly sophisticated setup.

That was on the Farewell Tour, which was in 2002 or 2003. It's hard for me to remember exactly what I had back then. [*Laughs.*] I was one of the first guys to use a Muse Receptor when they first came out, so I think I was using a couple of those. At that point I had a Korg Trinity and a Roland D-50, and then a whole bunch of Korg and Roland stuff in the rack with a MIDI switcher so I could change the whole configuration from song to song. That let me control any keyboard or module from any other keyboard or module.

What's you setup like now?

It's much simpler now. Right now I'm playing with Cher in Las Vegas and they want a lot of piano on this gig, so I'm playing a Roland V-Piano and on the top of that I have a Roland Fantom G-7 that controls a Muse Receptor, a V-Synth XT, a Nord Lead II rack module, and a Korg Triton rack module.

I like to layer things and you kind of need all of those modules to get some of the big synth-type layered sounds. In my mind, Korg has a totally different sound from Roland, even if they're trying to sound like the same thing. The Nord sounds like nothing else, and the Receptor has about 100,000 sounds in it from all the virtual instruments and samples that you can install. The palette is pretty much unlimited.

Are you doing fly dates, or are you in a bus?

With Cher we're only at Caesar's Palace in Las Vegas. Last year I was with Pink in Europe and Australia for part of the year. I didn't go out full-time with her, but I was out maybe about four months of the year. I had a rig that was bused from gig to gig, and we also had a duplicate rig in case there was somewhere that we had to go that was far away. Instead of busing the rig I normally use, we'd send the "B" rig on ahead.

How do you stay healthy on the road?

You have to treat road life as much as normal life as possible. Since my very early days on the road, I haven't been the kind of guy that would stay up and party all night. I've never been a big drinker, and I've never been a druggie or any of that. As I've gotten older, I've felt that was more for the kids new to the road.

Sometimes you finish a gig at 11 p.m., roll on the bus at 11:30, stay on the bus for four or five hours, then you have to get up and go to your room at five o'clock in the morning. It's hard to make that normal, but you still have to make sure that you exercise. Even if you haven't gotten much sleep, you have to try to get your butt out of bed and go to the gym.

You have to stay away from eating pizza every single night, unless you're 25 years old and still have the metabolism of a hummingbird. [Laughs.] The better shape you can keep your body and mind in, the better you're going to perform and play.

One of the things that's great about being on the road is that you travel to all these great cities where you can eat a lot of great food, party with your friends every now and then, and have a really great time. But you can't do that every night, because you're going to end up fat and lazy and not in very good shape. Eventually, it will take its toll no matter who you are.

What kind of things do you do for entertainment on the road?
I've always been one who tries to get out of the hotel as much as possible and see everything there is to see. You'd be surprised at the incredible places there are everywhere you go, so I've always been one to get out and see as much as possible.

I believe in spending every penny of my per diem. If I have a day off and I have to rent a car and it costs me more than my per diem, I'll do that if I have to. There's a great book that I got years ago when I first started touring called *A Thousand Places to See Before You Die*. Once we pulled into South Dakota and I saw something in the book called the Badlands. I never heard of the Badlands, but there they were right outside of town, so I rented a car and went out there and it's one of the most incredible places you've ever seen in your life.

So when I'm in a city and we're out in the middle of what seems to be nowhere, I'm going to go see whatever there is to see within 50 miles of where we're at, because who knows if I'll ever be in that place again? It's certainly better for my psyche to see something I've never seen before than looking at same hotel room I've been in a thousand times.

There are a lot of places where you see the same shopping mall over and over again unless you go out and really look for something else. It always drove me crazy when we'd be in Paris and there'd be guys that would get up and go to McDonald's. Why even be a musician on the road if you're not going to sample all the benefits it brings?

How do you pack to go on the road?
I always overpack because I like to have something available if I need it. I'm fortunate in that most of the touring that I've done has been at a pretty high level and there are always people to pick up your bags for you and move you around. I would probably still pack too much even if I had to move them around myself, because I like to be comfortable.

I take a lot of stuff. I take any and all clothes that I could possible want. I take a set of push-up bars and a couple of stretch bands, my PX90 [workout] stuff, and a few music books like some Bach, Mozart, and

Paul Mirkovich 227

Chopin that I can use for practice if I get some time. So I like to take as much stuff as I can so I can feel like I have everything I need.

How has touring changed from when you started to the way it is now?

The biggest change is in communications. Cell phones have revolutionized what we can do on the road in terms of how we can keep in touch with our family, friends, and business associates.

The other thing is that everyone now has a laptop. When I first went out in 1986, nobody carried a laptop with them anywhere. Now everyone has a laptop and an iPhone and maybe even an iPad with them at this point. Now, I can sit in a hotel room with my little portable digital audio system working on 3 gigs at once while I'm out on the road. That's a pretty remarkable thing. Even 11 or 12 years ago it was a nightmare trying to write music on the road.

Have you ever used a laptop as part of your rig?

Yeah, I was one of the first guys to use the laptop to play some VST synths before the Receptor came out. I used to run a few synths out of a software utility called V-Stack, which was very buggy and would crash all the time. Then the laptop would overheat and decide not to work. It was a pain in the butt, so I moved to the Receptor as soon as it came out. I have run tracks from laptops live on occasion, but I really don't like to be the guy pushing the buttons to run digital audio on a tour because I'd rather think about playing. But I have done it before on the two live TV series that I've done. It was a little scary but it worked.

Did you do it yourself, or did your tech do it?

On the TV show I did it because I was a little more comfortable doing it myself at the time, but I wouldn't do that now. I'd let someone else take care of it.

Before you go out, how much rehearsal time do you have?

It depends upon the gig. Usually for a major tour, it's six weeks of production rehearsals, plus I'll usually work with the artist for about a month before that to figure out what the show is going to be about. I'll write any incidental scene-change music, segways, intros and endings, the show beginning and ending, and that kind of stuff.

You're the MD on all the tours you do any more, right?

Yeah, I've been doing that since about after my first two years of touring.

I was pretty much an MD even before that, because people would make a mistake and they would ask me what they should be playing because I always knew everyone's parts. They would ask me, "Is this right?" so I naturally graduated into people asking me to MD.

What do you look for when you audition someone?

First off, I want the person auditioning to play the music exactly like the record. I don't want to hear them improvise, and I don't want to hear their take on it. I want to hear them play it exactly with the right feel, just like they were playing Mozart or Beethoven. I want them to respect the music regardless of if it's Pink's music, or Cher's, or Janet Jackson's, and I want them to play it exactly as you hear it on the record. Then if I ask them to change it, they're changing it from a place where I know that they know what it is, so they can take their own spin on it after the fact.

One thing I love to do to keyboard players is to say, "You're on stage and Pink is going to start this ballad. Play me 16 bars of an intro to this song before she comes out." You'd be surprised how many of them will play the most ridiculous shit. They'll play a lot of chord substitutions that don't fit with the music. It's a pop song with a one and a three and a five in the chord, and they're putting a seventh or a ninth on there and it's like, "What exactly are you playing?"

Sometimes I'll just say, "Just play me something. I don't care what it is," and they'll immediately go to the busiest, jazziest thing that they have. It's like, "Dude, this is a pop gig. I don't want to hear you play jazz. If the artist came right now she'd say, "What the hell is that?" So I'll walk over and I'll play something simple, like the Beatles' "Golden Slumbers," with just two fingers and the left hand barely moving, and I'll show it to them and say, "Just play that." If it were me, I'd watch how it was being played and play it right back exactly the same way, but most of the time they'll maybe get close, but the time will be all over the place. I don't care how many notes you can play—if you can't play them in the right time, it doesn't make a bit of difference.

A lot of times I'll find guys that are great jazz players who have no clue how to play something like simple pop. There's a right way and a wrong way to play anything, and that stuff is just as hard to play right as any other stuff.

I've been playing with Cher for 20 years and some of it is really simple music, and after a while the players begin to wander a bit. I always tell them before a show, "Let's play this show like it's the fourth or fifth time we've played it, not the 105th. Let's go back to square one and play it liked we originally learned it." There's a fan that comes in every night that can't wait for her to sing Gypsies, Tramps and Thieves, and as silly as that may seem to you or me, they've waited their entire life to hear her sing that song. If there's a bunch of shit all around it and it doesn't sound like the song they expected, they're going to go home disappointed. So that's the attitude you have to have when you go to play pop music. There's an art to how the producer and the artist put the song together and you have to respect it, unless they've asked you to change it. You can't just change it up because you're bored or you think that your idea is better.

Do you change your rig to suit the artist?

Nowadays, I don't go out long term with anybody any more. I'll go out on the first couple months of a tour. I set up a tour for other people to go out on, so I'll set up the rigs to what I think the keyboard players will need to play. As an MD I have a say over what everyone is using just because I know what horsepower we need to make the sounds for the gig, which means I also have some say in the guitar rig and the drum rig as well.

I have a relationship with a few different companies like Muse Research and Roland, so a lot of times I'm able to connect the tours with some of these companies that I work with. It's good for the companies and it's good for the tour because it's all good gear, but it all depends on what's needed on the particular tour.

Are you using in-ears?

Yeah. I hated them when I first started using them 11 years ago. I had the same reaction that everyone has during the first rehearsal, where you just want to fall down on the floor of the rehearsal space and cry because it just doesn't sound like anything that you're used to hearing. But once you get some subwoofers behind it and get used to hearing it, you can hear what everyone is playing so well, which is especially important for an MD.

I went back and did a tour a few years ago when I just used floor monitors and it was kind of a shock after running in-ears for so long. I also think it protects your hearing, too, as long as you don't run it too loud.

What kind of mix do you usually get?

I have a very complete mix in my ears. I can hear what everyone is doing almost like a record. I sing as well, so it's important that I can hear my own voice as well as what the other singers and the artist are doing.

Do you do anything to protect your voice while you're on the road?

If I'm on a tour that's very vocally demanding, I'll warm up early in the day and then again right before the show. I have a warm-up exercise that I do that I got from a voice teacher in L.A. named Roger Love. Other than that, I don't smoke and I drink lots of water. Smoking's like the worst thing that you can do for your voice.

I also try to make sure that I get enough sleep. If you're a singer, your body is your instrument so it has to stay rested.

What's the worst tour you were ever on?

I don't know if there's been an entire tour that's been horrible, because I've been mostly with pretty cool artists, but I've had some pretty horrible crew people out on the road with me. There was one tour where the tour manager was such a screwup that he went out on an all-night bender in Europe the night before we were supposed to leave to come home. He totally slept through getting all of our bags together and getting us all to the airport. He got fired that day. So I've been on tour with people that have been really bad at their job, especially one as important as that, which is pretty much of a drag.

There was one other time, where I told the artist that I was quitting on stage because his crew was so disorganized. Before a show one of the techs told me that I had to set up my own gear because they didn't have time to do it. Not that I'm a prima donna, but this is a tour and it's not my job to be setting up my gear in my stage clothes while the audience is staring at me. So I set up my gear and right before we walked on stage I told the artist, "This is my last gig with you. Thank you for the tour," and I went home right after that.

What do you look for in a tech?

I want a tech that is going to be as conscientious at the gig as I am. I expect whomever I'm working with to be really quick and to be listening to me all the time (especially during rehearsal), because if there's one thing that I hate, it's having to repeat myself. I expect them to get it the first time. I like someone who's knowledgeable at programming. I like to program all my own synths and stuff, but if I'm on the other side of the stage programming one of the other synths or if I'm in the front of house and I say, "Hey, can you bring the filter cutoff down?" I want them to know how to do that. Most of the guys I've worked with have been able to do it or at least figure it out pretty quickly. If they can't figure it out, then they're not there very long.

As far as an audio tech, because I do a lot of digital audio stuff too, I like them to be musical. If I say, "I need you to do this at the beginning of bar 6, beat 3," they know what I'm talking about. It's rare to find someone that musical, because if they are, they're usually playing with someone. But if you can get someone like that, it's a great thing.

What was the best gig you ever did?
Pink's gig in Australia last year was pretty sweet. A couple of years ago I played with Foreigner for about six months, and one of the gigs that we did was open up for Led Zeppelin at their reunion show. That was pretty phenomenal. Then I played at the White House once with Jeffery Osbourne, and that was pretty great as well.

Ed Wynne

One of the busiest musicians in Los Angeles, sax player, singer, and songwriter Ed Wynne keeps a hectic schedule both at home and on the road. Having played on a host of television shows, movies, and records, Ed cut his musical teeth on the road playing for a number of '50s acts, including the Platters, the Drifters, and the Coasters. Eventually, Ed found himself as the featured soloist with the Doobie Brothers, and is currently in the same position in Al McKay's All Stars, an Earth, Wind & Fire spin-off formed by its former members during the band's long hiatus. Ed has a long history of bus tours and fly dates all over the world, and he has plenty of tips and advice based on his experiences. Visit his website at www. edwynne.com for more information about him.

What was your first gig on the road?

I was 18 years old when I answered an ad out of the *Recycler* [an L.A. want-ad paper] and got a gig with a band called Danny and the Exciters. The first stop on the tour was Vegas, but it was eventually also supposed to go to Reno, Tahoe, and Atlantic City. Then by Christmas we were supposed to be down in Florida, where we were going to take a month off to rehearse and record an album, then go back on the road starting in Hawaii. That was what was promised, but I didn't know enough at the time to get it in writing.

233

Our first stop in Vegas was at the Palace Station, which at the time was the largest casino off the Strip. Since we weren't the headliner, we had to play six sets—at 8 p.m., 10 p.m., midnight, 2 a.m., 4 a.m., and 6 a.m. It was hell but I was 18, I was getting paid to be on the road, the food was free, and a bartender was getting me a few cocktails, so it was all good. Or so I thought. That's when I learned a few things about handshake deals, trusting people, and the value of covering your own ass.

What went wrong?
While we were playing at night, the MD and the artist were rehearsing a completely new band in the afternoon. At the end of the gig, we found out that they had already left for the next gig without us, and they didn't pay for our hotel rooms. They just left us cold at the Palace Station! To make matters worse, the Casino posted security guards on our rooms so we couldn't get our stuff back until we paid our bills. Needless to say, I came home with my tail firmly wedged between my legs.

What was the first gig where you felt you made it, or at least felt that you were in a pretty good place?
The weird thing you learn about the entertainment industry, especially the music business, is that if you ever mistakenly begin to feel that way, it doesn't last very long. A very brilliant guy that I met when I was 17 once said to me, "I don't care how much you know or who you're playing with, you just have to remember one thing—all gigs come to an end."

So it doesn't matter how high or how low you go. You have to approach it with a sense of humility and a sense of self-esteem, because who you are and how you're playing generally has very little to do with the gig you're on. Anybody can get a gig—the hardest part is keeping it. Most of touring is about personal interaction and making friends and not pissing people off. It has very little to do with how you play or where you went to school or any of that. It's the social aspect that's so important.

How often are you on the road these days?
It's about 50-50. I have four regular bands that I do in town, and then I have one main touring situation. The in-town situations that I play have to have trained, qualified subs ready to go in order for me to have the flexibility to be able to go on the road. It's a hard thing to

balance, because as players we all tend to mold the situation to our own skill set. You give a little bit more in an area where the other guy didn't or couldn't, so based upon your own personal skills, you become indispensable to certain gigs. While that makes it difficult to fire you, it also makes it difficult to find a qualified sub, so I've had to spend a great deal of time getting my sub situation together so I'm free enough to go on the road.

As far as being on the road, I started the year in Japan over Christmas and New Years. I got home on the January 2, and then I went to Europe the next day for a week. I came back for the middle couple of weeks in January, and then went to Europe for a week again. The last week in February, I went to Mauritius [an island off the east coast of Madagascar], and then I was home the whole month of April. Then in the first week of May, I went to the Seychelles Islands, which is another island off the coast of Africa. The Mauritius and the Seychelles gigs were one-offs. You fly halfway around the world to play one show, then turn around and come home. That was all with the Al McKay All Stars.

I remember seeing you with the Doobie Brothers. They featured you a lot. You were great.

Yeah, that was an interesting gig for a minute. I subbed for their regular sax player [Marc Russo] when he needed to have some personal time off. I only did the gig from April to August in 2002, but right now I'm at the point of my career where I'm still to this day known as "from the Doobie Brothers," and that was eight years ago. I think to myself, "Are you kidding me? That five months of my life is going to define me for the rest of my career?"

What are the most favorite gigs that you do? Is there a certain type of venue or style of music?

I have to take the Fifth on that one, because I don't have any. I absolutely passionately love what I do on any level. I don't care whether I'm playing a wedding, a club in a foreign country where the people don't speak English, or a festival for 100,000 people—I absolutely love what I do, and I have a good time no matter what.

Do you do many corporate gigs?

That's mostly what I do when I'm in town, but now the Al McKay band is starting to branch out into that. A lot of times what they'll do is book a private party at one place or another and then book a tour around that, using the bread from the larger-paying gig to pay for the flights and per diem and that kind of stuff.

The gigs in the Mauritius and Seychelles where both birthday parties, and the flights are 16½ hours from L.A. to Dubai, and then 6½ to Mauritius and 4½ to the Seychelles. You're talking about over 20 hours in the air, not counting all the security crap at both ends. The layover in Dubai to go to Mauritius was 9 more hours in the airport. We flew all the way out there to play a birthday party for some rich oil guy from Moscow who turned out to be a really cool, regular guy!

Did you turn around and come right back after the gig, or did you hang there for a while?
We came in a day early, so we had some time to get our wits about us and figure out what side of the planet we were on. Both times we had at least another day to relax and recoup before taking that brutal journey back home. The people that hired us were unusually cool, so it really wasn't too bad.

What kind of rehearsals do you usually get before a tour?
For the Doobies, they sent me show tapes of what the other guy was doing, because they were already in the middle of a tour. I studied those and learned my parts, then we had two days of rehearsals in Las Vegas before we played our first gig with me in the band. Then we played the Hilton Theater for a couple of nights. After each night I would get notes from the guys so I could tighten things up and figure out what they were looking for.

With Al McKay, when I first got in the band, we would have a week's worth of rehearsals before we went anywhere, just to make sure everything was tight. That was because every time the band would go out, there were four or five guys who had never done the gig before or hadn't done it in six months to a year. In order for it to be tight, you had to have a lot more rehearsals. Eight years later we might have had three rehearsals total in the last six months, and they were about two-hour run-throughs to make sure everything was up to speed because we had one or two new guys doing the gig. That's a product of the band being essentially the same for eight years now. It's supersolid, so when a new guy plugs in, they're plugging into a machine that's pretty dialed and ready to go.

When you go on the road, do you take the same instruments, or do you have "road instruments?"

I play the same horns on in-town gigs as on out-of-town gigs. There are a couple of reasons for that. One, I want to have a consistent sound no matter where I'm playing, because you never know who is going to hear you, who is going to be in the audience, and where your next referral or contact is going to come from. I don't want to be anywhere in the world and not feel comfortable with my setup, my sound, the intonation, and all of the things that go into a professional-level performance.

When you do a fly date, do you carry your instruments on the plane with you, or do you check them?

It depends on the gig. If I'm just playing tenor, I will carry it on in like a Walt Johnson lightweight flight case. The reality of air travel now is that they can and will take your instrument away from you and you have to be prepared for the fact that it might end up in the baggage compartment of the plane. So on a single horn gig, I would carry that horn on. Now Al McKay's band is an alto and tenor gig, so I had a custom flight case made that fits both horns that's both undersized and underweight when it's loaded with everything in it. It weighs 49 pounds, which is one pound under limit, and it's also under the size limitations so I can check it like a regular bag and there are no problems. I've had that road case now for five years and it's served me very well. It got nailed once and I had to have the top panel replaced, but even with a big gouge in it, the horns were still perfect.

I was putting my alto in a Walt Johnson case and putting that in my suitcase, and then carrying my tenor in a Pro Tec case. What happened was we got over to Europe and we were taking these little puddle jumpers [small planes] where there was only enough overhead space for a briefcase, and they took the tenor away from me and put it in with the other baggage. When I got it back it was destroyed, and I had a show that night.

What did you do?

I might be one of the luckiest guys on Earth, because the promoter was also a sax player who called the local repair guy for me. Then he personally took my tenor over to him, and when I got it back it played better than when I put it in the case. So I ended up playing the show on my own horn that night.

So that made me realize that I can't take that chance ever again, because even though the planets all aligned this time around, that doesn't mean that it's ever going to happen again. As soon as we got back, I went and got my road case.

Fast-forward to the very first time I took my case on the road: it missed the connection and didn't show up to the gig. I had to borrow horns, borrow mouthpieces, borrow everything for that show. What I learned from that was not to check my mouthpieces, reeds, neck straps, and all that stuff. I now pack them in a little bag in my carry-on. Because they're metal and they're pointy, I get stopped everywhere, so I leave a reed on it so I can blow through it for Security so they understand what it is. Because I do that, if I get someplace and the horns don't make it or they're damaged, then I can get a better sound out of a borrowed horn as long as I have my mouthpieces and reeds with me.

What extra do you take with you? Is there anything special?

I always have an extra neck for each horn. That's one of the things that will get destroyed by drunk people all over the world. A horn will start to fall and they'll grab it around the mouthpiece or neck like it's a handle to stop its fall. I've seen the neck get almost twisted off the horn as a result. So I have an extra neck for each horn in my road case.

Do you ever have trouble hearing yourself on stage?

With Al McKay's band, the horn section uses in-ears, so I rely on the monitor engineer to be able to hear myself. We've had a few situations where we've had some RF problems so the in-ears didn't work properly, but there'll always be some wedges on the floor just in case something like that comes up. Frequently, the wedges aren't loud enough for me to hear myself over the band, so in cases like that I'll take one in-ear out so I can hear myself and the band acoustically, and leave the other in my ear in case the in-ear mix starts to get better as we go along. That also blocks some of the sound from the brass. The gig is two trumpets, trombone, and saxophone, so the brass is playing about four times louder than the saxophone. If I leave in the in-ear that's pointed towards the brass in my ear, I can hear myself better.

Do you all have the same mix, or are they separate?

That depends upon the venue. Ninety percent of the time, the trombone and the tenor have one mix and the two trumpets have another when the wedges are shared, but every time we use the in-ears on a gig, we have individual mixes.

Do you bring your own mics?

I bring an Electro-Voice clip-on microphone specially designed for wireless transmitters. For solos, we want to use a wireless as much as possible, so we can bring the soloist to the front of the stage to interact with the crowd and that kind of stuff. This mic is compatible with the wireless packs that are supplied by the sound company. Some of the mics that come with the wireless packs don't sound that good in my opinion, so this gives me something that I know will sound good and be consistent from gig to gig. When I'm playing with the rest of the horn section, I just use the mic that's on the stand.

I used to carry some other mics with me, but I stopped doing that in order to keep everything below the minimum weight so I didn't have to pay any extra fees.

Do you have any tips for auditioning?

I personally haven't done one since I auditioned for Frankie Valli's band in 2001, but I tell people to remember that a big part of the audition is about how you got there in the first place. They're going to view you differently if you were referred by somebody in the band or management, or if you just heard about it and showed up to an open cattle call. Everything is based on their preconceived ideas of who you are, who you know, and what gigs you've done, so if you keep that in mind, you're probably going to be less disappointed in the outcome.

The other thing is that you have to not only be better than everyone else, but you have to be different. It's basically a sales pitch. In five or ten minutes, you have to prove to them that if they hire you, they'll get more for their money than hiring anybody else. If you sing as well as play, they should know that, so you should figure out a way to work that in. If you play percussion, even if it's just cowbell and tambourine, bring it and set it on the ground right next to you so it's easy to pick it up and play if it's appropriate. Even it you don't play it at the audition, they'll have an idea that you have that capability.

The way I got the Frankie Valli gig was they made us sight-read some charts and we sounded pretty good. But while the powers-that-be were talking amongst themselves, I looked at the next chart and said to the guys, "When we get to this section, we're going to do this step." I choreographed a little step that would put us in front of the mic when we played, and away from the mics when we weren't. So we danced like we were choreographed while we sight-read the tune, and that's how I got the gig. It had nothing to do with my endorsements or credits or who I knew (I didn't know anybody on this particular gig— it was an open audition), but I got the gig by doing something above and beyond the call of duty. I got them thinking, "If this is how they are sight-reading at an audition, can you imagine how much they'll add to the show?"

That's one of the mistakes that musicians generally make. Most of what we do has very little to do with playing, but has everything to do with entertainment. If most musicians could keep the entertainment and sales side of the business on their minds, they would work more and they would probably do a better job in most situations.

Do you have any tips for staying healthy on the road?
Yeah. First and foremost, you can never drink too much water, and the less alcohol you drink on planes, the better. Even though getting a nice light buzz might seem to make the flight go faster, alcohol dehydrates you and you get off the plane feeling a little bit weak and even a little disoriented. People think it's because they're tired, but most of the time it's because they're dehydrated.

I also take PowerBars or some kind of nutritional bar on the road with me, because you can't depend upon other people for your sustenance on the road. I've been stuck before when we've missed our flight and nobody had any money for food, so I learned never to go out on the road broke. Always take a credit card so if you get stuck anyplace and your gig blows up, you're able to get home. It's the same thing with food. Don't let anyone stick you on an eight-hour bus ride on a sit-up bus with no food and no water where they're telling you, "We can't stop because we don't have the time. We're going to miss soundcheck as it is." While that may be true, you have to take care of yourself, so when you get on the bus, take a bottle of water and a couple of PowerBars. If they stop for lunch, great. If they don't, you're still covered.

It sounds like you've been doing a lot more fly dates than bus tours these days.
Well, we'll fly to Europe and then we may have a sit-up bus or a sleeper bus, depending upon how long the rides are. We did 33 days where we flew to Europe, and for most of the tour we had a sleeper bus, so I've done both.

In my early days, I did a lot of the "ten guys in a van with a trailer full of gear" stuff. I did that with the Platters, the Coasters, the Drifters, the Cadillacs, and all those '50s and '60s acts that had horns when I was in my late teens and early 20s.

How about some tips for the bus? How do you entertain yourself?
I know this is going to sound really old-school, but I always bring a book because sometimes when you're on the bus with a lot people crammed in, the chances of having some kind of unpleasant discourse between band members or management or crew is pretty high. The longer you're out, the less sleep you have, and the more you see the differences in personalities. It's inevitable that there's going to be a blowup. I always want to have an escape or a self-defense to get out of those social situations which can go bad and lead you to losing your gig. Burying yourself in a book is a good way to stay out of those situations.

Then I take a lot of electronic distractions like a laptop, a PSP (which you can set up to get your email and load music onto), and an iPod. I also generally bring work with me, because I usually have things to do like transcribe horn parts for an upcoming gig, do some arrangements for a recording session, and things like that. When I don't have anything like that to do, I'll sit down and write a game plan for when I get home. A lot of times your head gets clear because you're away from the day-to-day grind of trying to make a living in town, so you get a different perspective on everything. You start remembering all those marketing things that you used to do that you haven't done in a long time, so I'll make a list of goals and ideas that I can do to help my business when I get back in town.

How do you balance your life on the road with your family life?
That's the hardest one, because as musicians we're pretty much programmed for when the phone rings, you go do the gig. Nothing is more important than the gig, so when you throw in the wife and family and all that goes with it, you have to try really hard to balance it all.

There are certain things I won't do. I won't miss my wedding anniversary, and if I'm going to be on the road when it happens, I fly my wife out to be with me. It's only once a year, so it's a small price to pay and it really does go a long, long way. I won't miss graduations, either. I have two sons, and the only times I've missed gigs is when my kids graduated from different schools. I won't miss those occasions, because they're the kind of things that you can never go back and fix down the road.

How do you approach soundcheck? Is there something that you specifically want to work on during soundcheck?
Yeah, I want to work on getting back to my room. *[Laughs.]* The reality of a soundcheck is it's not for you unless you're the artist. The soundcheck is about making other people happy, and the sooner you realize that it's not about you, the less frustrated you're going to be.

The most important thing you can do for soundcheck is to make friends with the monitor engineer. If you make friends with him, he's going to go out of his way to make sure that you're happy, Then, it doesn't matter if you show up at soundcheck or not. Buy him a bottle of Jack, thank him for working so hard, grieve with him that he's underpaid (because they always are), and that will go a long way. He'll go way farther for you than if you show up at soundcheck going, "I can't hear myself!" *[Makes a crying sound.]*

Being a monitor engineer is a hard gig because there's always someone unhappy, and most of those people are farther up the food chain of the gig than you are. The most important guy on the stage is the bandleader. If he's not the lead singer, then the lead singer is next, so already you're fighting for third place if you're really, really lucky. In Al McKay's band, the lead trumpet player has been with Al for over 30 years, so he might get ten minutes at the check all for himself, and he's earned that. I would look like a real jerk if I made the soundcheck all about me.

Socially speaking, soundcheck can be a really good way of losing your job. I've seen it happen to guys that complain too much. It's starts with, "I can't hear myself," and then it escalates to include other people's stage volume and how they have to turn down for you, and it can spiral out of control really quickly from there. Then you throw in the fact that everyone is jet lagged, you've had three hours of sleep, and you're halfway around the world, and you can see how tempers can flare in no time.

What do you pack when you're going out? Do you take anything special?
There are certain things that don't leave my suitcase when I'm home. I'll always take a 220-to-110-volt power converter. That comes in

handy even in another 110-volt country because sometimes you'll be backstage at a venue trying to get power, and all you can find is a 220-volt drop when you need to charge your cell phone. The second thing is a short two-foot power strip, because there never seems to be enough outlets to charge all the electronic devices that you travel with.

I also take sunscreen and mosquito spray everywhere. The other thing I do before I leave is to check with my doctor if I'm going somewhere that I've never been before to find out if there are any travel or health alerts. About one out of every three times, my doctor says there is. You have to check to make sure that you're not walking into some sort of epidemic or a disease that we've conquered here but they haven't conquered yet where you're going. You certainly don't want to bring it home to your family.

As far as clothes, you're always checking the weather for where you're going, because just because it's warm where you're at doesn't mean anything. Generally, no matter how long I'm going out of town, I don't take more than a week's worth of clothes. More than that and the suitcase gets too heavy and then you'll be overweight, which depending upon the kind of tour you're on, you might end up paying the excess weight charge yourself. I'll take sample sizes of detergent and just wash my clothes in the sink. If you lay them in a towel and just walk across it a few times, the towel absorbs most of the moisture. If you then hang the clothes up in the bathroom overnight, they're generally dry in the morning, with the exception of jeans.

You have to get your frequent-flyer stuff and your hotel-points thing together, because these are perks that you can get and share with your family when you get home. This way, your family can reap some of the benefits of you being gone.

We had a tour that ended in France, so I flew my wife and son out to Paris on frequent-flyer miles and we stayed in Paris for a week on hotel points. The entire week maybe cost only $500 or $600 that was spent on food. So perks like that will help you balance the family with the touring, but you have to be organized to take advantage of it.

Another thing, whenever you get your itinerary, don't trust a travel agent to get you the right seat, because you can bet that you're going to show up to the airport and find that you're stuck in a middle seat. You don't want to take a long flight in the middle seat, especially when you're traveling to Europe or someplace even farther. When you get your confirmation number, call the airline or go online with your frequent-flyer number, because if you're Silver or Gold or Elite class, that's going to help you rearrange your seat assignment. You'll have priority over someone who doesn't fly as much. Don't rely on other people to do what you can do for yourself.

What was the worst road experience you ever had?
Wow, I don't know that I can break that down into one instance. There are so many rotten things that have happened over the years, and most of them were nobody's fault. The first tour in Vegas that I told you about was pretty bad.

The first time I went to Europe with Al McKay's band, we flew from L.A. to San Francisco, then onto Charles De Gaulle airport in Paris where we sat for five hours waiting for the bandleader and tour manager to show up. When they finally showed, we got on a bus and drove across Paris to Paris Orly airport, then flew to Tunisia, had a two-hour bus ride to the venue, and played that night! At that point I felt like, "If this is touring, I might think about flipping hamburgers."

I have tons of road stories, but all tours are not like that at all. I don't want people to think that it's miserable, because it's really not. I've been doing this a long time and I keep doing it. I've put a lot of miles in. and these are the exceptions and not the rule.

What was the best gig you ever did? Is there one that sticks in your mind?
To me, that's like [trying to figure out what was] the worst gig, because of all the gigs that went wrong, there's even more that went right. It has to be that way, or you'd stop touring.

I played the Power of Freedom Festival in Houston on July 4, 2002, with the Doobie Brothers. They estimated that there was between 50,000 to 100,000 people in the audience, and it was a live network broadcast at the same time. That was a pretty great gig.

With Al McKay we've played some great places like Casablanca, Tunisia, Moscow about ten times, and the Montreux Jazz Festival, which was amazing. The funny part is, I've met more of L.A.'s top musicians while on the road in foreign countries that I ever have here.

Glossary

220-volt drop: A 220 volt power outlet.

ADD: Stands for "attention deficit disorder," a condition in which a person becomes easily distracted and has trouble focusing.

ATA road case: A road case that follows the specifications developed by the Airline Transportation Association and specifies the manner in which a case is built so that it will survive at least 100 plane trips.

axe: Another name for "instrument," mostly referring to guitars.

B-3: A model of Hammond organ preferred by many musicians for its sound. A- and C-type models are essentially the same as the B-3, except for the cabinet.

backline: Band gear that's usually placed to the rear of the stage, consisting of drums and amplifiers. Sometimes keyboards are also considered backline.

baffle board: The piece of wood in an amplifier or speaker cabinet that the speaker or speakers are attached to.

boffin: A person who has very specific technical knowledge.

chart: the sheet music for a song. It may be note for note or only an outline of the form with specific passages written out.

DAW: Stands for "digital audio workstation," which houses computer software for music recording.

day room: A hotel room booked just for the day so the band can relax before the gig, usually from 9 a.m. to 6 p.m.

day sheet: A daily memo that every tour member receives, telling them the events for the upcoming day and when they will occur.

deck: The stage.

dolly: A type of carrier with handles that, among other things, facilitates moving instruments like a Hammond organ.

doors: The time when the doors of the venue will open to allow the audience in.

dress rehearsal: The last rehearsal before a show; it is usually run without stops or interruptions.

float: Extra money that the tour manager carries to help cover emergencies.

flight case: A transportation container specially reinforced to safely transport items needing protection. Some cases have advanced protection in order to survive the rigors of multiple airline flights (see "ATA road case" and "road case").

fly date: A show that you fly to, and then return soon after the show ends.

festival: Usually held outdoors, a music festival brings together a number of acts that sometimes perform over a period of days.

Floyd Rose: A brand of guitar vibrato bar that allows extreme string bending.

front of house: Also called "FOH," this is the sound system that the audience in a venue will hear.

Grand Ole Opry: A weekly radio show based out of Nashville that has presented the biggest stars in country music since 1925. It's the longest-running radio show in history.

guitar vault: A road case that allows multiple guitars to be transported. It also functions as a guitar stand for each guitar during the show.

hang: To socialize.

in-ears: Short for "in-ear monitors." A custom-molded earpiece similar to ear buds that allows the performer to hear a monitor mix without using floor monitors.

in-store: A promotional stop at a record store (or any type of store that sells music) that involves signing autographs or playing a short set.

IEC cable: An international standard cable used for plugging a device into standard AC power.

insert: A jack on a console that allows the engineer to insert a piece of outboard audio gear into the circuit. Sometimes found on guitar amps, it can be used to insert an effects device between the preamp and the power amp section for cleaner operation.

intermittent: An unexplained crackling or on/off operation that sometimes happens with electronic instruments.

layered guitars: Multiple overdubbed guitars; commonly found on rock and pop songs.

lead: Another word for the cable that connects a guitar to an amplifier or effects.

Leslie speaker: A cabinet with rotating speakers, usually used with an organ. Most Leslies have a rotating high-frequency speaker, and a drum inside the cabinet that rotates around a low-frequency speaker that gives the sound a unique Doppler-like effect.

lift: A European name for an elevator.

load-in: The scheduled time for when equipment is loaded into a venue.

Loctite: A thread-locking fluid that holds a screw in place, and can be used instead of a washer.

machine heads: The mechanical winders on the head of a guitar that tighten or loosen the strings. Sometimes called "tuners."

MD: Stands for "musical director."

microfiber cloth: Preferred for its light weight, super absorbency, and ability to dry quickly, one strand is 10 times finer than silk and 100 times thinner than a human hair.

MIDI: Stands for Musical Instrument Digital Interface. An industry standard protocol that allows electronic instruments, controllers, and devices to communicate with one another.

MIDI assignment: A configuration of MIDI messages.

minibar: A small refrigerator found in some hotel rooms that is stocked with beverages and snacks. It's checked every day by housekeeping, and the user is charged for all items that are consumed.

monitor system: A speaker system that allows a musician to better hear himself and the other players onstage. Most monitor systems have a number of customizable mixes for different members of the band so that they can perform at a higher level.

multimeter: An electronic meter that measures voltage, current, and continuity that's used for testing and measuring.

Murphy's Law: An adage that states, "Whatever can go wrong, will go wrong."

musical director: The bandleader (see also "MD").

nut stock: The material to make a nut, which is a small strip of bone, plastic, brass, graphite, stainless steel, or other medium-hard material that sits at the joint where the headstock meets the fretboard. Its grooves guide the strings onto the fretboard, giving consistent lateral string placement.

one-off: A single show, after which you return home.

P Bass: The short term for "Precision Bass," a bass model made by Fender.

patch: A customized preset, when referring to electronic keyboards. The word comes from the early days of synthesizers, when the way a synth sounded was determined by how its modules where physically connected through a series of cables.

per diem: The money paid for daily meals when on the road.

phantom power: External power supplied to condenser microphones, which need phantom power to operate. The power may come from a mixing console or a dedicated power supply.

piezoelectric: A material that generates an electrical signal as a result of pressure. A type of transducer used in instrument pickups.

pots: Short for "potentiometer," the electronic name for the rotary volume and tone controls on guitars and amplifiers.

promo tour: A tour of television and radio appearances and in-store performances by a musical artist to promote a new album.

rider: an addendum to a contract to perform that's a list of requirements provided by the artist to the promoter.

road case: See "flight case."

RF problem: A radio frequency interference problem, which is usually caused by the local police or fireman radio transmitters, and their disruption of the use of wireless systems.

shed: A venue that's an outdoor open-air covered pavilion.

shedding: short for "woodshedding," a term originally used by jazz players which means to go off and privately practice.

side-fill: Speakers on the sides of the stage that have a more complete mix of the band than do the monitor mixes.

SIM card: A subscriber identity module" (SIM) is a removable electronic card that stores a service subscriber key used to identify a mobile-phone subscriber.

sit-up bus: A bus like a city transit or school bus that has no amenities for touring.

Skype: A software application that allows users to make voice calls over the Internet.

sleeper bus: A bus with sleeping facilities. A tour bus.

soundcheck: A short run-through by the artist or band about three hours before the show to check that all production gear is working and that everyone is comfortable with the sounds and levels.

speaker simulator: A rack-mounted box that takes the place of a speaker. A guitar player can get the sound he's used to having by supplying the resulting signal to the mixing engineer, who plays it back in the monitors. This keeps the onstage volume minimal.

splits: To divide a keyboard into different sections, with each section having a different sound.

Strat: Short for "Stratocaster," a popular Fender electric guitar.

thermal shock: When an instrument is brought in from the cold and immediately warmed up, it may suffer from thermal shock, which can warp a wooden instrument or cause its finish to crack.

timecode: An electronic form of metadata added to film or video to identify the precise time of each frame. Although used mostly during film and video editing, it's also essential for synchronizing sound and lighting effects to video playback.

tines: In a vintage electric piano like those made by Rhodes and Wurlitzer, the tine is the part that is struck when a key is depressed, and that makes the sound.

tour bus: A specially adapted bus used primarily to transport artists, bands, and their crew and technicians from show to show. Sometimes known as a "sleeper bus" or an "entertainment coach."

TSA: Stands for Transportation Security Administration. The security people at airports who screen for prohibited items for airline travel.

variac: A device that varies the AC line voltage either up or down.

venue: A place where an organized event like a concert occurs.

virtual instrument: A software simulation of an instrument that's run from a computer. Virtual instruments include drums, synthesizers, piano, organ, bass, as well as other instruments.

wedge: A floor monitor with a wedge shape that points up at the musician.

wireless channel: Wireless systems for microphones and instruments can be thought of as a small radio station, needing a transmitter and a receiver to operate. Each wireless transmitter and receiver requires its own frequency, or channel, in order to receive the output of only that one instrument or microphone.

wireless unit: A wireless transmitter and receiver.

wireless transmitter: A unit that's either built into a microphone or comes as a separate belt-pack and is used to transmit the wireless signal to a receiver that is placed near a mixing console or an amplifier.

Woodstock: A musical festival held in 1969 on a farm outside of Bethel, New York (ironically, 43 miles away from the town of Woodstock), and is widely regarded as a pivotal moment in music history. As a result of the attendance of more than 500,000 people, music from that point on became a big business.

workbox: A large road case containing most of the spares that a player might need on the road. It also includes a workbench.

Index